Copyright © 2019 by Sophia Jane Tucker

Website: sophiatucker.com

Email: info@sophiatucker.com

ISBN: 9781798976005

First published in Great Britain in 2019 by Tapestry of Beauty

All rights reserved. No part of this publication may be reproduced or distributed in any form or by any means, or stored in a database or retrieval system, without the prior written permission of the author.

Unless otherwise indicated, all Scripture quotations marked (NKJV) are from the New King James Version ®.
Copyright © 1982 by Thomas Nelson. Used by permission. All rights reserved.

Word studies conducted using Strongest Strong's Exhaustive Concordance of the Bible, The: 21st Century Edition ®
Copyright © 2001 by Zondervan. Used by permission. All rights reserved.

All emphases in scripture quotations are added by the author.

Cover by Matthew Tucker

MW01169536

RENEWING THE MIND 101

A practical guide and devotional of how to renew the mind

By Sophia Tucker

FOREWORD

In these last days Father God is urging His body to mature, to grow up and to become all that God has called it to be. For the children of God to rise up and to be manifest as His sons and daughters; it will take a corporate push of a collective renewing of our minds. This is why this book is so important.

I have personally experienced the power of renewing the mind in my own life and have seen God's will mightily demonstrated on many occasion and lives changed as a result.

It has been my honour and privilege to witness such an incredible transformation in Sophia's mind and heart; she has grown from strength to strength, risen from brokenness and uncertainty to a place that is stable and grounded.

There is an only proverb that states: if you give a man a fish; he won't go hungry that day, but if you give him the knowledge and skills to catch fish, he won't go hungry for the rest of his life. I firmly believe this is what is offered through this book, it comes from years of experience and actually walking it out, living it out, this is not only theory, this is not merely practice, this is from a life outpoured, from having resisted unto blood, and from the depths of the pit to the heights of breakthrough.

Sophia Tucker is well equipped to share the tools and equipment needed for renewing the mind. The totality of this study is a compilation of sorts over the years, gleaned from direct instruction from the Holy Spirit, years of diligent study and application, the truth of His Holy word and inspiration from many blessed ministers of our Lord who have also poured out of their lives to strengthen the body of Christ.

I am proud to be a part of this journey also and proud to say to you that this book contains precious keys of breakthrough that when applied consistently will revolutionize the way you think, speak and live. Renewing the mind 101 isn't just for you; it is for everybody who wants to build their lives. We can do so in such a way that we won't have to wait for the next big conference to renew our minds, we won't need to wait till the following Sunday, or a Wednesday group to be topped up, but every day can be a glorious power packed period of spiritual growth and renewal. My friends and family in the Kingdom, we can do this, you can do this, and as we do, we will begin to live a life that causes His kingdom to come and His will to be done, on earth as it is in heaven.

As a husband, a brother in Christ, and as a man of God, I fully endorse Sophia Tucker as a voice crying out in the wilderness that God is raising up in these last days.

Be attentive to hear the voice of the Holy Spirit as you read and follow along with the faith actions, receive the unction of the call; to make straight the paths of your mind for God to move through. So as a final word, use this book exhaustively and get everything you can out of it and my brethren, your life will never be the same.

Foreword by Pastor Evangelist Matthew Tucker

ACKNOWLEDGEMENTS

I want to acknowledge my Heavenly Father who has been so patient with me over the years. This journey has been years in the making with His mighty hand guiding me every step of the way. I stand in faith and belief that as He asked me to write this book that it will fulfill its purpose as it has been in mine.

I praise God for my beloved husband, Matthew. Your late nights and early mornings both helping me get this book edited and proofed as well as your hours standing with me in countless prayer and support has been like no other. Thank you for holding me through nights of pain and sorrow and rejoicing with me in Gods mighty victory. You are a true inspiration. Thank you for laying down your life for me as Christ does for the church.

To my sons, one day you will read this, and you won't remember all the sacrifices that were made to put this into place. But I praise God that as you grow in the Lord that you will continue to fulfill the God-given design for your life.

Thank you to Sarah Cooper. I prayed to the Lord He would send me a sister in Christ that would be my kindred in what we believe and desire going hard after God. He divinely connected us. Not only that but your countless hours in prayer and helping encourage me to write this in times when I did not think I could. Thank you for praying with me when all the challenges came in. Thank you for all the scripture prayers! Thank you – Love x

Thank you to Barbara Robbins for being a wonderful accountability partner and going through life's ups and downs together. Also, I am so thankful for the help in proofreading this study x

To the TFT/Tapestry Group leaders & members, Thank you for being my family and thank you for believing, praying, encouraging and standing in the gap. Judith, Susan, Robbie & Carol thank you, thank you, thank you!

Thank you to my parents, grandparents, Aunties, Uncles and spiritual parents who helped build a true and solid foundation in my life. Mummy Stella who I miss greatly but I know who is interceding for me in heaven.

Thank you to my sisters Sonia and Sarah that have always encouraged me to go hard after my goals and always believing in me.

Thank you, Barb Raveling, for your encouragement, wisdom, and advice.

I want to give honour to the great teachers that I have learned from on renewing the mind; Barb Raveling, Rev Curry R.Blake, Julie Blair, Paul Brown, Pete Cabrera Jr, Mike Bickle, Beth Moore, Dr. Caroline Leaf and of course my husband Pastor Evangelist Matthew Tucker.

HOW TO COMPLETE THIS STUDY

You may have tried renewing the mind before or maybe you are an expert, either way, this study may be different to the way you have practiced before. However, I want to tell you that renewing the mind is intensive. Therefore, the way I have designed the guide is to build progressively throughout the weeks ahead.

I have tried many methods and ways of renewing the mind and the ones that I saw the most significant transformation from required; time, focused dedication and concentration.

I hope that the reason you acquired this book is not just to read and study about renewing the mind but to dig deep and put it into practice. I am here with you every step of the way. I have compiled this program with much prayer and guidance from the Holy Spirit so that it will bring great transformation in your life.

How long?

This study will run for a total of 63 days (9 weeks). Scientifically 21 days of renewing our mind can start to bring about change but consistently renewing the mind for 63 days on any area can establish a new mindset into the core of a person.

What will we be doing?

Each week there will be the main topic that we will be covering to discover more about who we are in Christ, renewing the mind and the tools for mind renewal transformation. Each day you will read a section of this book and complete the Bible study questions, speak biblical affirmations and pray scripture prayers. Also you will complete the designed renewing the mind plan. You can see an overview of all the weekly tasks in the Appendix.

Renewing the Mind Plan

I have designed a daily mind renewal plan for you to complete and you can find this at the beginning of each new week of the study.

As well as having your daily quiet time with the Lord, completing this Bible study you will need to complete the renewing the mind plan. These are suggestions of a method that has worked for me and I hope for you also.

Daily Assignments

Each day will be a renewing of the mind daily assignment these should take 20 minutes but take as long as you feel the Lord is leading you.

Faith Actions

Faith actions are steps you will take every day to cement truths and be a doer of the word and not just merely a hearer. Here you will enquire of the Lord for what He is leading you to do each day and write in your accountability form/journal). These should typically be short and to the point – but let the Lord lead you.

Repeating Faith actions 7 times a day (set an alarm) –

This is so important! You want to take the faith action and put a reminder in your phone. This is going to reinforce your new truths in a consistent and focused manner which is so vital for a renewed mind.

You can also download the renewing the mind tracker to help keep you accountable as well as other resources from www.sophiatucker.com/RTM-101-resources

Mountains

We are going to seek God in prayer to pick a mountain that He wants us to renew our minds about (In Week 3) and start renewing our minds on that area over the remaining several weeks using the tools in this book. I believe that this a personal decision between you and God. Through prayer, He will reveal this area to you. Or maybe He already has before starting this study. Either way, we are going to walk together through this daily and submit everything to the Lord.

Resources you will need

Daily

- The "Renewing the Mind Trackers"
- A journal
- Your Bible
- A phone/app you can set alarms with ('JustReminder' is an excellent app for this)

Weekly

- There will be resources mentioned throughout this book, you can find these in the Appendix or on the website.

Video Support/Additional Support

- Throughout the study, there will be video's to watch to support you on this journey. You can find these on my YouTube Channel
- Additional Resources can downloaded from my website www.sophiatucker.com as well as the Appendix of this book.
- If you need personal support or have any questions, please email me on info@sophiatucker.com

WEEK ONE

RENEWING THE MIND 101

Week One Daily Plan (Days 1-7)

Week one begins with us renewing our minds on renewing our minds. It sounds funny, but if we don't take this first vital step the remainder of the journey will be difficult. You need to know why you are renewing the mind and the power there is through the Word of God as you are going to want to hold on to these truths. I know you probably really want to address your area of renewal and that will come in week 3, but take these first critical steps this week and next week, and we will genuinely be laying down some great foundations.

Each day

Quiet Time with the Lord

- Make sure you have your usual time with the Lord daily

Bible Study

- Read days 1 - 4 and complete the Bible study questions
- Days 5 - 7 speak all the daily affirmations & scripture prayers

Renewing the Mind Daily Suggestions

- Before you start, gather any materials or printables you are going to need

- Before you start mind renewal each day take a few moments in thanksgiving for what God is going to do in you as you renew your mind.

- At the end of each mind renewal session write down any revelations you received from the Lord in your personal journal or the mind renewal weekly tracker.

- Set the alarm for a minimum of 7 times a day ideally every hour and have armed with you scriptures that you are going to meditate on. You can also do your faith actions in these times.

- Before you go to bed take a scripture and meditate on this and see yourself in that scripture.

Renewing the Mind Daily Plan – Week One

- This week we will be focusing on meditating on "Renewing the mind" truths.
- In the appendix, you will see a list of affirmations on renewing the mind.
- **Days 1-7** each day take the time to slowly read through 5 of the affirmations/scriptures.
- Next, you are going to speak these out loud.
- Take the affirmations/scriptures and ask the Lord to reveal to you how He wants you to apply these in your life.

Faith Actions

- What action of faith is the Lord asking you to do today? This could be praying a scripture prayer or speaking out some affirmations.

Do your faith action 7 times a day.

WEEK 1

RENEWING THE MIND 101

Day 1

"When you became born again you have become a new creature. (2 Corinthians 5:17) Just as the same can be said for a caterpillar in its metamorphosis state when it fully transforms into a new creature – the butterfly. You had the genetics of this world, but now, you have the genetics of heaven and you are joined as one with the Lord."

-Sophia Tucker

INTRODUCTION

Thank you for taking the time to read and follow along with this study on Renewing the Mind 101. No matter where you are in your life, renewing your mind to the Word of God is the key to real transformation. When we take the time, focus and dedication to bring God's word and apply it to our minds and lives, the breakthrough is genuinely available to us.

Over the last few years I've been greatly blessed because of how God has moved powerfully in my life and those around me. I can testify that the results are undeniable.

In this study – through the use of daily assignments – we will be looking at a variety of different methods that we can use to renew our minds. Over the next nine weeks, we will take each method and work hard to apply these practices to our lives. Everyone likes to renew their mind in certain ways, and that's fine, some of you may wish to try all of the methods and utilize them for different situations that you are facing right now.

We will start by taking 1 area (mountain) the Holy Spirit leads you to renew your mind on. It may be food idolatry, anger, a marital issue, or only just learning to embrace renewing the mind itself as something you must include as a lifestyle. There will be daily assignments for you to complete to support you in the mind renewal process, along with a critical topic, tool or aspect of renewing the mind.

My heart is that you will find the answer to the questions I often get asked "How do I renew my mind *exactly?* How often? And when is the best time?" Etc.

MY TESTIMONY

I want to share a testimony about when I had been in a severe battlefield in the area of anxiety. I noticed over some time that I would find myself crying while going about everyday life around the house. I had always struggled at times with anxiety and in fact before I became saved I suffered from clinical depression.
So I was well versed on this from previous experiences. But this time it was different.

I ignored the signs
Unfortunately, I mostly ignored these thoughts of fear even though I had a better than beginners knowledge of renewing the mind. One day I started having breathing difficulties that caught me off guard, and I was taken to the hospital.

While I did have some iron issues which could have contributed, the doctor said to me that I was suffering from anxiety. I brushed it off in annoyance and frankly I was offended. But then other family members including my husband mentioned that I had been stressed lately. I again grew angrier and hurt by the thought of this.
But days later I slipped into a seemingly never-ending stream of panic attacks that caused me not to be able to look after my family or home. Every night for about 2 or 3 days I was either in a hospital or with an ambulance crew with us at our house.

The Breaking Point
I spent many nights physically shaking and getting no sleep because of the severity of the panic attacks. I was exhausted in every possible way. I had reached a point of complete brokenness.
I was prescribed some medication, but I knew that the effects would be harmful for me, let alone the side effects! The thought alone had me terrified and panic-stricken.

I made a choice
So one Sunday morning I was faced with the decision to go and pick up the prescription or go to a local church my husband advised, for me to receive counsel & prayer. We climbed into the car, and my husband drove to me towards the hospital – I knew that there was a chance that if I took the medication I would become numb and my children would no longer recognize their mummy anymore.
As my husband drove on praying loudly and declared God's word fiercely, he urged me to go God's way. Having come to the end of myself, it was then that I said to God in tears and panic "I have to trust You, I don't know how you can get me out of this, but I have

no choice but to try!" I soon noticed that we had entirely driven past the hospital.

Thank God for the Body of Christ!

I went to the local church and lo and behold they were teaching on taking thoughts captive! After the service, the minister gave me a CD and said "you need to speak these truths about who you are in Christ; you have to immerse yourself in this fully. This is not the life you have to live you have a purpose. Now fight! Keep declaring the truth no matter how you're feeling or what the enemy is speaking." He prayed a powerful prayer for me.

The Battlefield

I went home and felt like I could slightly breathe better. The only way I could describe all that was going on inside me was that I felt like I was in prison within my mind and in my body at the same time. My mind didn't feel all there; it was like a constant foggy and dazed feeling. I still could not eat or sleep and it got to the point where I couldn't walk. Any natural calming methods made things worse.

Fully immersed

From that night on and for several days after with the help of my husband and praying close family, I spent every day in my room for more than 72 hours declaring the word of God, meditating, worshiping, journaling all the scriptures and revelations I was receiving, listening to worship music, sleeping/dreaming. I was blessed that all of my household and parenting duties were taken care of.

It may sound like I had a great time to rest and relax, but I tell you it was not. It was a life or death battle and fight to the very end, every step of the way. I had to be obedient and go against what my mind and body wanted to do. I had to eat when I didn't want to as the Lord led. I had to get up and try to walk when my body was weak from muscles I had not been using. I had to get to a point where even when all my family left, and my husband had no choice but to return to work, that I could believe that I would be able to cope. At the same time, I grew closer to the Lord than I had ever been and realized that this was going to be the beginning of something that would not only help me but help others too.

How did I get here?

I must add... I knew quite a bit about renewing the mind – if I had not, I don't think I would have gotten through. However, I learned more about the intensity and the consistency that is necessary when having to overcome such a crisis of faith, aka my mountain that I needed to have moved.

I asked the Lord, "why, why did I go through this?" There were many things I experienced that year and even things resurfacing from my past. Was it the betrayal of a friend? Was it the challenges at my husband's place of work? Was it the pressures of being a home-school mother? Or was it past trauma? The image I saw was just a deep chasm with no floor. The Lord revealed to me that there is no root cause; these things happened to me and are common to all men. (1 Corinthians 10:13) But hallelujah! We serve a mighty God, and He makes a way in the wilderness and has indeed already made a way.

The Beginning of Transformation

The answer shocked me. God's revelation hit my soul with these words:

I had not yet learned how to take my thoughts captive effectively.

This was the beginning of my transformation. I became hungry and desired to study and understand in greater depth, renewing the mind and taking thoughts captive. I praise God that after five days of this most crucial battle, I was finally free from these panic attacks, I could return to a new normal.

My life would not be the same.

I made it my mission that after having gone through this trauma, I would use it as fuel to help prevent others from going around the same mountain as I have; be it the same, similar, or perhaps even worse. Whatever your mountain is that you have to move, there is healing for you along the path to victory, and I can promise you this; defeat is never Gods will for any of His children. All things are possible; you can win!

SCRIPTURE PRAYER

Father, I immerse myself in your teaching and meditate on them always. Your Word has become so real in my life that it bares fruit and everyone can see my progress. I give careful attention to my spiritual life and cherish every truth, for living by Your Word releases an even more abundant life inside me. I am continually being renewed in the spirit of my mind; I put on my new self, created after Your likeness in true righteousness and holiness."
1 Timothy 4:15-16, Ephesians 4:23-24

AFFIRMATION

Father, You are the source of perfect peace: You will keep me in perfect peace because my mind is fixed on you; because I place my confidence in you. Isaiah 26:3

WEEK 1

RENEWING THE MIND 101

Day 2

WHY WE SHOULD RENEW OUR MINDS?

For many years I heard about renewing the mind but did not understand what that meant, what it looked like, or even the discipline that is required to do it effectively. I probably thought that I was renewing my mind by applying basic Christian practices.

I praise God for His Grace; He indeed has helped me in significant ways to put off the old and put on the new. But there were so many gaps, and I didn't understand why I did not have lasting change in my life in certain critical areas. I kept on going round and round the same mountains for many years just like the Israelites. My journey started with one of those mountains when I wanted to find ways to lose weight through a 100% godly manner.

This led me to studies by Barb Raveling. Through growing to understand the power of renewing the mind in this area, I for the first time in my life found a breakthrough, which impacted so many other areas of my life. But it was not an easy journey; in fact, I struggled to truly understand why and how to do this. I went on the journey of study and leaning on God's Word. I had to renew my mind about renewing the mind. It was an uphill struggle for me, and my flesh did not want to know. The first step for all of us is to understand why we have to renew our minds to line up with the Word of God and why this is critical to our walk with God, in Christ Jesus our Lord.

What is renewing the mind?

Renewing of the mind is a tool given to us by the Lord to indeed change our lives through the complete transformation of our thinking, attitudes, and views of life. Nowhere else in the bible does it promise that believers can have their lives transformed other than through the renewing of the mind. Renewing the mind is a complete renovation of the mind of a Christian; it is the proactive removal of information and mindsets that do not line up with the Word of God/mind of Christ.

We can live in a beautiful, harmonious state of mind that will allow us to think in the same way Christ thinks. God had a perfect plan for all His children, but because of the Fall, His plan was interrupted. However, through the Power of Christ, our mind can be restored to operate as was originally intended.

The Battlefield

"Mind Renewal is getting rid of all the unbelief so that you will not be double-minded and can walk in pure faith."

- Reverend Curry Blake

Unfortunately, there is a mighty war that goes on between the flesh and the spirit which causes us to be double minded. The bible says that when we are doubleminded, we can't receive anything from the Lord. It is due to unbelief in our hearts causing us to doubt whether the word of God is true or not. Renewing the mind is a process that removes unbelief so we can eradicate being double minded and walk in great faith.

The Mind is Powerful

Recently, I was watching an interview with an actor who said that to prepare for his role in a movie playing a villain; he began by isolating himself from all friends, family and the love they would bring. He won many awards for this movie but afterward when trying to reintegrate into society he could not do it as he felt that he was still that villain and this caused depression and required therapy. The mind is extremely powerful. Anyone can condition themselves to believe and act in a certain way. This man clearly was able to look back and see how drastically he had changed. How we think can truly change our brain.

But praise the Lord the Word of God is the only powerful tool that can divide between soul and spirit and can truly transform us according to the Fathers purposes. We have the Holy Spirit that can permeate every part of our mind to aid us in this spiritual process.

No matter what mountain you are facing today you can begin the change approved by God that makes that very mountain be brought down low and utterly destroyed.

SCRIPTURE PRAYER

I thank You, Lord that as I meditate on your word that my soul prospers and this means that every area of my life will prosper as I stay focused on You and Your precious truths. My heart is full of thanksgiving.

3 John 1:2

AFFIRMATION

The Word is the final authority in my life. God said it, I believe it. It is settled in my life.

BIBLE STUDY QUESTIONS

➢ Have you tried mind renewal before? If so, what areas of renewing the mind are unclear to you?

➢ When thoughts come to your mind, do you ever wonder if they are your thoughts or if they have come from God or the devil? How can we distinguish if they are our thoughts, God's thoughts, or if they have come from the enemy?

➢ Why do you think we need to renew our minds?

WEEK 1

RENEWING THE MIND 101

Day 3

BE TRANSFORMED!

I want to take a moment to talk to you about being in a place of transformation. It is often an area that many believe they cannot attain, or believe it's God's will to stay in the same battles of life over and over again. It is not His will for you; His promises and His Word are true.

You can live transformed!

You have to experience transformation so that it does not become all about you and your life, but we are called to be Christ's representatives on this Earth. Renewing the mind is not self-improvement; it is self-actualization. Knowing the truth of who we in Christ is the goal. From that place, we can act and live out for others the way God has called us to.

Butterflies & Caterpillars

With renewing the mind, we are going through a variety of stages and with different goals. Just like the process of metamorphosis of a caterpillar to a butterfly, each stage has a different purpose.

Stage 1: Egg & Caterpillar

In the caterpillar's 1st stage of life, their main focus is to eat so they can grow quickly. When they are tiny, they cannot travel far, so it needs to eat from the leaf it is born on. The mother butterfly will only lay her eggs on the right type of leaf the caterpillar needs to feed off. When the caterpillar grows their skin does not stretch, but they do grow by molting (shedding the outgrown skin) several times. A caterpillar can only see basic variances in light but cannot see images.

In the beginning stages of renewing the mind, the key is to take in the word of God about a particular toxic thought/mountain that the Lord wants us to focus on. We don't change physically straight away on the outside, but as we immerse ourselves several times a day in the truth, our mind is shedding off lies. However, our vision is still limited.

Stage 2: Chrysalis

Resting stage – from the outside of a Chrysalis it looks like a caterpillar is resting, but this is where all the action is truly taking place. Inside, the caterpillar is rapidly changing and all the old parts are being broken down and are completely changed by the end of the cycle.

For us in the renewing process, is where the real work also takes place. It's a time of resting in Christ; however we are also proactively transformed as we deny our former opinions and attitudes that do not line up with who we are. The goal here is to rest in Christ.

Stage 3: Butterfly

At this stage, the butterfly has to come out of the Chrysalis their form is from the confines of the Pupa. They then have to rest after all the work. After several hours they master flying, and the final goal is to reproduce. The butterfly has excellent vision and can see patterns and images that the caterpillar could not see and even humans cannot see with 15 different types of sensors. Butterflies and Caterpillars don't just look different; they behave differently also.

When we have gone through the process of mind renewal, we come out walking and talking as God intended.

Not only are we very different our next goal is to reproduce. This can take the form of reproducing this process in taking down another mountain, but also, now we are free to not only help others overcome the same mountains we now have freedom in, but we are also more able and available to know and do the will of God in other areas too.

If you are plagued with constant battles in the mind and despair takes up so much of your time then you need to make the shift into the mind of Christ. I cannot tell you how many years I dealt with fear and anxiety but I can say it was too many and took over many areas of my life. There is no condemnation here however, and I have fully seen God redeem the time.

An un-renewed mind and toxic thoughts block the purposes of God coming to pass in your life. This is something the enemy wants.

➤ What would your life look like once transformed in the area you will be focusing on?

Let's go back to the foundation scriptures:

Romans 12:1

I beseech[a] you, therefore, brethren, by the mercies of God, that you present your bodies a living sacrifice, holy, acceptable to God, which is your [b]reasonable service. ² And do not be conformed to this world, but be transformed by the renewing of your mind, that you may prove what is that good and acceptable and perfect will of God.

Ephesians 4:21-30

²¹ if indeed you have heard Him and have been taught by Him, as the truth is in Jesus: ²² that you put off, concerning your former conduct, the old man which grows corrupt according to the deceitful lusts, ²³ and be renewed in the spirit of your mind, ²⁴ and that you put on the new man which was created according to God, in true righteousness and holiness.

- The task is to be transformed by destroying the former old man conduct and renew our minds to the truth.
- The aim is to become living proof of the manifestation of the Word of God.
- The call is to become a living sacrifice.
- The purpose is truly knowing the will of God and living it out.
- The way is by living through the mind that Christ has made available for us.
- The commission is to reach the lost and make disciples.

SCRIPTURE PRAYER

My Heavenly Father, thank you that I can present my body as a living sacrifice. Let everything I do with my body be a holy and acceptable love gift to you, because of your great mercy. I worship you, I love you, Jesus... you are my Lord. Holy Spirit you help me to renew my mind so that I will not live a life that reflects the world, but a transformed life that reflects heaven. This mind we build together in partnership, will know what the will of God is, which is always good, acceptable and perfect.
Romans 12:1-2

AFFIRMATION

Every promise You have made I stand firm in them and in the overflow of confidence I stand in peace and strength.

WEEK 1

RENEWING THE MIND 101

Day 4

SPENDING TIME WITH GOD

Beloved, there is a key that is often understated when it comes to renewing the mind. It is the importance of cultivating the discipline of spending time with the Lord. Today we are going to focus on these areas. They include prayer, abiding in the Word, fasting & silence/waiting on the Lord.

Prayer

Prayer and intercession connect us in divine fellowship with the Lord.

Often when we engage on the journey of renewing the mind, a surprising and often overlooked area is prayer. It is critical that we understand that fellowship with the Lord is vital! Do you have a prayer plan? I believe without a plan we may pray, but we will pray a lot more with a dedicated and focused strategy.

It is essential to partner with God in this process; after all, He is the one that does the transforming work in our heart.

Philippians 2:13
¹³ for it is God who works in you both to will and to do for His good pleasure.

I used to say that "I am renewing my mind but why does it seem not to be working as effectively as I would like?" In Philippians 2:13 it shows that it is God who works in us to do His good pleasure/will. Fellowship with God is the catalyst we need to get us to a greater degree of transformation.

Prayer & renewing the mind both enables us to know the will of the Father.

1 John 5:14 shows us where our confidence is in prayer.

1 John 5:14

14 Now, this is the confidence that we have in Him, that if we ask anything according to His will, He hears us.

Silence

"Silence is golden" is more than a proverbial saying. Whether we are praying, studying God's Word, or renewing our mind, silence is a necessary discipline. Most of us live such busy lives that it is near impossible for us to be silent and to hear the voice of God. Building a regular time to be still before the Lord is another practice that will pay high dividends. You may find this hard at first, so I recommend instrumental worship and then start with 5 minutes of silence and listening. Use a notepad and pen to write down what you have heard. Even if you think it's your thoughts, still write them down.

Assignment

➢ If you do not already have a scheduled time for prayer or reading the Word, then please plan sometime in your schedule to allow for this. Also, carve out some time in the mornings to ensure you are completing the mind renewal plan.

➢ During this study, I would recommend you have a prayer time for a minimum of 20 – 30 minutes in the morning and time with the Lord before bed. If you pray more than this, then please continue with your plan.

Abiding in the Word

The Bible teaches us that the Word is Jesus. Once I received a vision that the Holy Spirit was connecting my heart to the heart of the Father. I received that this comes through not just prayer but abiding in the Word. Jesus is the manifested Word. The Word of God has within it the DNA of God.

John 6:63

It is the Spirit who gives life; the flesh profits nothing. The words that I speak to you are spirit, and they are life.

John 15:7 also talks about us abiding. When we abide in the Word, we are divinely connected to his purposes for us, His will and mind.

Friends when we spend time in the Word it is a powerful tool in the renewing of the mind.

I love pray-reading scriptures as I commune and talk with God. I will talk about this more in week 3. But let's take the time today to commit to adding in dedicated prayer time. In the Appendix is a daily schedule. Today I want you to put in times that you can spend in prayer and reading.

Fasting

I want to take the time to make a note on Fasting. I could write a whole book on fasting, but I want to encourage you that personally, I and so many others have found great breakthrough through fasting. Some mountains in our lives need the power of fasting to catapult us out of some problematic strongholds. We remember Jesus saying that this will only come out through prayer and fasting. Fasting breaks the strongholds and the yolks. I believe in the power of fasting and creating a lifestyle of fasting not just once a year, but a weekly/monthly basis is very beneficial. It makes me sensitive to the words that God desires to speak into my life and future.

Worship

I would not be able to finish this section without discussing worship. Worship to God opens our heart and prepares us for great intimacy with the One we truly love and adore. As a worship leader for many years, some of my most amazing times of sweet fellowship have come from giving adoration and exaltation to the King. I want to mention here that one of the ways I renew my mind is by singing scripture back to the Lord. Many of the worship songs we sing today are purely from the scriptures.

Colossians 3:16

Let the word of Christ dwell in you richly, teaching and admonishing one another in all wisdom, singing psalms and hymns and spiritual songs, with thankfulness in your hearts to God.

SCRIPTURE PRAYER

Father, I have confidence and great boldness that I can come before You and ask anything according to Your will. You will hear me. And You will continually revitalize me, implanting within me the passion for doing what pleases You. Because I live my life in union with You and Your words live powerfully within me—I know I can ask whatever I desire and it will accomplished.

1 John 5:14 , Philippians 2:13, John 15:7

AFFIRMATION

I am personally experiencing the love of God; therefore, I look through His eyes at every situation with total peace

BIBLE STUDY QUESTIONS

➢ Why is cultivating a relationship with God through spiritual disciplines important to you? Which specific practices are you currently using, and which new disciplines will you commit to begin?

➢ Do you think it would be beneficial to have a plan for prayer? If so how could you implement this?

➢ Read 1 John 5:14. God wants to do a transformation in your heart. Why do you think He wants this for you?

➢ Why do you think practicing silence before God is important?

➢ What steps can you take to implement that today?

➢ Why does the flesh profit us nothing?

➢ John 15:7 Talks about abiding. What does this mean to you? Observe the keywords.

➢ What is the best time to pray do you think? Do you think you pray enough?

WEEK 1

RENEWING THE MIND 101

Day 5 – 7

Take the time over the next few days to read through and pray these affirmations and scriptures from during the week. Don't forget to do the daily mind renewal plan.

SCRIPTURE PRAYERS

Father, I immerse myself in your teachings and meditate on them always. Your Word has become so real in my life that it bears fruit and everyone can see my progress. I give careful attention to my spiritual life and cherish every truth, for living by Your Word releases an even more abundant life inside me. I am continually being renewed in the spirit of my mind; I put on my new self, created after Your likeness in true righteousness and holiness."

Father, I have confidence and great boldness that I can come before You and ask anything according to Your will. You will hear me. And You will continually revitalize me, implanting within me the passion for doing what pleases You. Because I live my life in union with You and Your words live powerfully within me—I know I can ask whatever I desire and it will be done.

I thank you, Lord that as I meditate on your word that my soul prospers and this means that every area of my life will thrive as I stay focused on You and your precious truths. My heart is full of thanksgiving.

My Heavenly Father, thank you that I can present my body as a living sacrifice. Let everything I do with my body be a holy and acceptable love gift to you, because of your great mercy. I worship you, I love you, Jesus… you are my Lord. Holy Spirit you help me to renew my mind so that I will not live a life that reflects the world, but a transformed life that reflects heaven. This mind we build together in partnership, will know what the will of God is, which is always good, acceptable and perfect.

AFFIRMATIONS

Father, You are the source of perfect peace: You will keep me in complete peace because my mind is fixed on you; because I place my confidence in you.

Every promise You have made I stand strong in them and in the overflow of confidence I stand in peace and strength.

I am personally experiencing the love of God; therefore, I look through His eyes at every situation with total peace.

The Word is the final authority in my life. God said it, I believe it. It is settled in my life.

WEEK TWO

IDENTITY 101

Week Two Daily Plan (Days 8-14)

This week we will be renewing our minds on identity. This is very important as it is difficult to renew our minds effectively if we do not know who we are in Christ. Next week we will be addressing personal mountains and therefore this week is a great way to prepare. So take some time to pray and ask the Lord what He is asking you to renew your mind on from Week 3 onwards.

Quiet Time with the Lord

- Make sure you have your usual time with the Lord daily

Bible Study

- Read days 8-11 and complete the Bible study questions
- Days 12-14 speak all the daily affirmations & scripture prayers

Renewing the Mind Daily Suggestions

- Before you start, gather any materials or printables you are going to need

- Before you start mind renewal each day take a few moments in thanksgiving for what God is going to do in you as you renew your mind.

- At the end of each mind renewal session write down any revelations you received from the Lord in your personal journal or the mind renewal weekly tracker.

- Set the alarm for a minimum of 7 times a day ideally every hour and have armed with you scriptures that you are going to meditate on. You can also do your faith actions in these times.

- Before you go to bed take a scripture and meditate on this and see yourself in that scripture.

Renewing the Mind Daily Plan – Week Two

- This week we will be focusing on meditating on "Identity in Christ" truths
- In the appendix, you will see a list of affirmations & scriptures on identity.
- **Days 8-14** Each day take the time to read through 5 scriptures/affirmations slowly
- Next, you are going to speak these out loud
- Take the verses and ask the Lord to reveal to you how He wants you to apply THEM in your life

Faith Actions

- What action of faith is the Lord asking you to do today? This could be praying a scripture prayer or speaking out some affirmations.
- Do your faith action 7 times a day.

WEEK 2

IDENTITY 101

Day 8

WHO YOU ARE IN CHRIST

If we do not know who we are in Christ, honestly, renewing the mind fully in other areas is going to be very difficult and in many ways fruitless. Renewing the mind with a wrong knowledge of our son-ship in God in my humble opinion is potentially dangerous. Many times we learn from well-meaning teachings or doctrines which unfortunately do not line up with the word of God. The Bible teaches that in the end days there will be false doctrine and false teachers so we must be on guard and know the reason for why we believe. You must test every word and be a student of the word yourself and learn to divide the word correctly.

When you became born again, you have become a new creature. (2 Corinthians 5:17) Just as the same can be said for a caterpillar once it has metamorphosed, it has fully transformed into a new creature – the butterfly.

You had the genetics of this world, but now, you have the genetics of heaven and you are joined as one with the Lord.

Romans 8:9
⁹ But you are not in the flesh but in the Spirit if indeed the Spirit of God dwells in you. Now if anyone does not have the Spirit of Christ, he is not His.

1 Thessalonians 5:23
²³ Now may the God of peace Himself sanctify[a] you completely; and may your whole spirit, soul, and body be preserved blameless at the coming of our Lord Jesus Christ.

Hebrews 4:12
[12] For the word of God is living and powerful, and sharper than any two-edged sword, piercing even to the division of soul and spirit, and of joints and marrow, and is a discerner of the thoughts and intents of the heart.

There are three main parts of our human nature, Spirit, Soul, and Body. Below is a chart to explain the main points.

Spirit	Soul	Body
Communicates with God and is God-conscious	Will, Emotions, Conscience, memories	Touch, Taste, Smell, Sight & Hearing
It holds the fullness of God	Choice, Intellect, Reason	Is World Conscious
The Glory of God resides in this place where we hold our First Love.	Mind (subconscious, Conscious)	1 Corinthians 3:1-3
Here is where we operate in Revelation, Intuition, Prayer, Reverence, Faith, Hope, Worship and Fear of God 1 Corinthians 2:11	1 Corinthians 2:14	

When we were born naturally, we were taught how to perceive life from the five senses of our body which then impacted our soul, determining our life decisions and choices. Our spirits were darkened being born into a carnal nature which is under sin.

BIBLE STUDY QUESTIONS

➢ Do you have a strong understanding of your identity in Christ? Why do you think it is essential for you on this journey to comprehend who you are in Christ?

➢ Romans 8:9 Identifies that we are no longer in the flesh. But why do you think that so often some believer's life decisions characterize the nature of the flesh?

SCRIPTURE PRAYER

Father, I cast off the old sinful nature, which was never your will for me anyway. I do not belong to this world any longer; I am a citizen of heaven. I am led by the Holy Spirit and have set aside all jealousy and quarrelsome attitudes. I have learned to walk in your spirit and have found maturity in Christ.

Corinthians 3:1-3

AFFIRMATION

I am the temple of the Living God, and You take delight in me and who I am. It is your enjoyment to commune with me.

WEEK 2

IDENTITY 101

Day 9

THE CARNAL MIND

There are two types of mind-sets that we need to acknowledge there is the Carnal/Natural mind and there is a Spirit-Led mind/mind of Christ.

Today we are going to focus in on the carnal mind.

The carnal/natural mind is directed to focus on the natural or carnal things. The reason for this is because the senses of the physical body influence the priorities of the carnal mind and this mixed with soulish carnality aims to dictate our actions and habits. It is a place which leads us to make fleshly and earthly decisions with great enjoyment to the flesh but is often mixed with great sorrow, regret, pain and in the end, darkness. It is a place led by feelings, circumstances and believing the world's perspectives and answers to life's issues. Unfortunately many people profess Christ and say they believe the scriptures, but still, live and act in a carnal manner.

Many Christians are living a life far below the position and authority God has given them.

Natural wisdom and logic is often their guide and often view other Christians who are completely abandoning their life to Christ as having gone too far. Some believe that; if you are too heavenly minded, you are no earthly good when in fact the opposite is true. The more heavenly minded you become the more earthly good you will be.

James 3:13 -18 clearly shows us that there are two types of wisdom and the evidence of how developed these types of wisdom are operating in your life, can be measured against the criteria listed below in the following verses.

James 3:13-18

[13] Who is wise and understanding among you? Let him show by good conduct that his works are done in the meekness of wisdom. [14] But if you have bitter envy and [h]self-seeking in your hearts, do not boast and lie against the truth. [15] This wisdom does not descend from above but is earthly, sensual, demonic. [16] For where envy and self-seeking exist, confusion and every evil thing are there. [17] But the wisdom that is from above is first pure, then peaceable, gentle, willing to yield, full of mercy and good fruits, without partiality and without hypocrisy. [18] Now the fruit of righteousness is sown in peace by those who make peace.

Romans 8:6

[6] For to be carnally minded is death, but to be spiritually minded is life and peace.

When we walk in a carnally minded way, this leads us to a place of unbelief, fear, lack, unrest, torment, confusion and death. This is not God's will for us. We have been bought with a precious price, and we need to turn around full 180 and line ourselves up with our new nature.

1 Corinthians 2:14-16

The natural man does not accept the things that come from the Spirit of God. For they are foolishness to him, and he cannot understand them, because they are spiritually discerned. The spiritual man judges all things, but he himself is not subject to anyone's judgment. "For who has known the mind of the Lord, so as to instruct Him?" But we have the mind of Christ.

The above scripture lets us see that a carnal man or someone who walks in the natural or fleshly mind, cannot comprehend the things that come from Holy Spirit, but hallelujah, those who walk in the spirit, (that's you and me) we HAVE the mind of Christ.

BIBLE STUDY QUESTIONS

➢ What do you think the dangers are of being too earthly minded? Do you think it is negative to be too heavenly minded?

➢ Where should your mind be fixed according to the scriptures?

➢ Looking at the two types of wisdom. Where do you think you sit? What steps do you need to take to lean more towards wisdom from above?

SCRIPTURE PRAYER

I thank You, Father, that I do not walk as a natural man any longer, but I am a spirit and a child of the Most High. I can hear your truths and judge righteously. The natural man cannot know the mind of the Lord but my old man is dead, and I have the mind of Christ. I can understand all your ways. In Jesus' name, Amen

1 Corinthians 2:14-16

AFFIRMATION

I shall not be known after the flesh but my Spirit. I refer to my spirit and not my efforts, abilities nor circumstances.

WEEK 2

IDENTITY 101

Day 10

WHAT IS THE MIND OF CHRIST

As born again believers we now have the mind of Christ available to us. However, it is our choice to believe the Word of God or believe the ways of the world, which are influenced by the deceptions and strongholds of the enemy.

However, even though we have the mind of Christ available to us, we have to train ourselves to walk, live, think and act the way He (Christ) does.

It goes against who Christ is when we still believe, live and think in a state that was meant only for the unsaved. Before we were saved, it was completely acceptable to see a troubling situation and worry or have doubt when things don't line up to how we expected. It was normal when faced with a mountain to think it is impossible to overcome. However for those of us who are in Christ these beliefs directly contradict the Word of God. Because He promises He will never leave or forsake us and He loves us with love like no other. Our task here is just one, and that is to BELIEVE!

John 6:28-29

Then they said to Him, "What shall we do, that we may work the works of God?"

Jesus answered and said to them, "This is the work of God, that you believe in Him whom He sent."

John 3:18
"He who <u>believes</u> in Him is not condemned..."

Mark 5:36
"... Do not be afraid; only <u>believe</u>." (NKJV)

What is a mindset?

A specific way of thinking: defining a person's attitude or set of opinions about something. A mental inclination, habit, or tendency. A predisposition.

The choice here is that we can decide what particular way of thinking we want to align ourselves with. But let's look at the truth of what is available to us.

1 Corinthians 2:16
[16] For "who has known the mind of the LORD that he may instruct Him?" But we have the mind of Christ.

Philippians 2:5-7
[5] Let this mind be in you which was also in Christ Jesus, [6] who, being in the form of God, did not consider it [a]robbery to be equal with God, [7] but [b]made Himself of no reputation, taking the form of a bondservant, and coming in the likeness of men.

Philippians 3:15
[15] Therefore let us, as many as are mature, have this mind; and if in anything you think otherwise, God will reveal even this to you.

We can now hear from Christ. We can know His ways, thoughts and walk in obedience to His beliefs; this means we can have victory in our lives. We have Jesus' mind in us, and His Word richly abides in us.

When we gave our lives to the Lord, we died and gave up our opinions and rights. He now lives in us. Our mind is the area that was not immediately transformed but requires a process. So the responsibility we have now is to line our minds up with the truth that resonates in and through our very core.

The key to knowing who we are in Christ is that we have to be assured that we believe in Jesus, the living Word and that He is true, the Word is true.

Standing in the truth of who we are is not an easy task, but we have to entirely abandon ourselves to Him and trust that the Word is the final authority over all our circumstances.

One of the most powerful first steps to transformation is to choose to change your mind from the world's views, values, and opinions which create the same hopeless and destructive results over and over again. Or, you have to decide to believe and walk in the Truth of the Word of God and His kingdom, which creates the Jesus Christ kind of results over and over again: love, joy, peace, patience, goodness, kindness, faith, gentleness, self-discipline. Our life can be filled with hope and victory.

Deuteronomy 30:15-16
[15] **"See, I have set before you today life and good, death and evil, [16] in that I command you today to love the LORD your God, to walk in His ways, and to keep His commandments, His statutes, and His judgments, that you may live and multiply; and the LORD, your God, will bless you in the land which you go to possess.**

Jesus only spoke those things that He heard the Father speak and taught what the Father taught. We would do best to live by the same.

What does the mind of Christ look like?

The mind of Christ is so unlimited but below are just a few examples of it in action.

The mind of Christ is Bold –Acts 1-:38, Matthew 8:16

The mind of Christ fears nothing – Luke 8:30

The mind of Christ moves mountains – Mark 11:20-24

The mind of Christ forgives all – Matthew 6:15, 9:5-7, Ephesians 1:7

The mind of Christ sets the captives free – Mark 10:45-52, John 1:17, Luke 4:18

The mind of Christ speaks those things which are not as though they were – Romans 4:17, Hebrews 11:3

ASSIGNMENT

Today open your bible and read the above scriptures regarding what the mind of Christ is like.

THE NEW COVENANT

Hebrews 10:16
"This is the covenant that I will make with them after those days, says the LORD: I will put My laws into their hearts, and in their minds, I will write them,"

Hebrews 8:10
10 For this is the covenant that I will make with the house of Israel after those days, says the LORD: I will put My laws in their mind and write them on their hearts, and I will be their God, and they shall be My people.

SELAH MOMENT – Take a moment here to praise God and thank Him for what He has done for you.

Many have given their lives to Christ and rejoice that they have been saved from going to hell. But the Lord has a reward for you here and now, which means that we can live in total victory. We can walk in peace and hope now! You don't have to wait grinning and bearing through life's struggles until you reach the sweet by and by. We want to graduate from the milk of the word, the 101 basics of Christianity and move to a place of reigning in this life victoriously (Romans 5:17). My heart grieves as I see so many brothers and sisters living in pain and turmoil. YOU DO NOT HAVE TO! Don't settle for only just being saved by grace but still living like the world in every other way. You were created for a purpose, so rise child of God!

GREAT NEWS!

Jesus has given us His mind; we can see and think the way He does. Well, we may say how? I don't feel like I have the mind of

Christ. Exactly! This is where renewing our mind comes in. We have to renew our mind to the mind of Christ. The result of renewing our mind should lead us to the point where we think, act, make decisions, and talk like Jesus and bring forth fruit just like Jesus wills for us to.

John 15:16
[16] You did not choose Me, but I chose you and appointed you that you should go and bear fruit and that your fruit should remain, that whatever you ask the Father in My name He may give you.

To have the mind of Christ means His thoughts can become our thoughts, His ways can become our ways; His ideas can become our ideas so that we can automatically respond like Jesus would in any given situation.

This, my friend, is Great News! We HAVE the mind of Christ! Now we have to renew our mind so that the mind of Christ is made manifest in our everyday life.

SCRIPTURE PRAYER

Thank you, Jesus that I have the mind of Christ, thank you that You have given me this gift. I can now think like you and talk like you and live the way You want me to live. Reveal to me what area you want me to work on over this study. I commit this time solely and entirely to You and trust that I can experience a breakthrough in this area. You are my faithful God; there is none like you.

DAILY AFFIRMATION

It is no longer I who lives but Christ who lives in me. I have the mind of Christ and will walk in righteousness before my God.

WEEK 2

IDENTITY 101

Day 11

SPIRITUAL WARFARE

The enemy's chief target is the mind because the most effective way to influence behavior is to influence thinking. Our minds are the control centers of our entire beings. – Beth Moore (Praying God's Word)

2 Corinthians 10:3-5

For though we live in the flesh, we do not wage war according to the flesh. The weapons of our warfare are not the weapons of the world. Instead, they have divine power to demolish strongholds. We tear down arguments, and every presumption set up against the knowledge of God, and we take captive every thought to make it obedient to Christ. And we will be ready to punish every act of disobedience, as soon as your obedience is complete.

We are in a WAR! The battles in our mind that we face are because we are in a spiritual war. Many are not aware of this truth and often think it is them and go through certain situations needlessly, while the tools of the renewing the mind has been given to us to overcome these battles and experience life-long transformation.

Our old man/mind has been warped to believe the lies of this world, the enemy and our previous fallen state. God has commissioned us to be soldiers in this war but not by natural earthly weapons. We must take up His divine power to TEAR Down arguments, every OPINION or thought that goes against GOD'S thoughts. WE HAVE TO TAKE THEM CAPTIVE. You HAVE TO punish every act of disobedience that your flesh wants to operate in until it's entirely in line with obedience to God's Word.

To take captive - to lower (or with violence) demolish (literally or figuratively): KJV – cast (pull, put, and take) down, destroy.

When we look at the Greek definition, we have to do this with force and violence. This is not easy but necessary if we want to see a change in our lives.

BIBLE STUDY QUESTIONS

➤ Did you know that the translation of to take captive is defined with such powerful terms as "demolish," "violence" and "destroy"? What image does that bring to mind?

➤ Do you think you have been renewing your mind with that mindset? How can you apply this to your mind renewal journey?

SCRIPTURE PRAYER

Father, I thank you for the revelation that for although I live in the natural realm, I don't wage a military campaign employing human weapons, using manipulation to achieve my aims. Instead, my spiritual weapons are energized with divine power to dismantle strongholds effectively. I can demolish every deceptive imagination that opposes God and breaks through every arrogant attitude that is raised in defiance of Your true knowledge. I capture, like prisoners of war, every thought and insist that it bow in obedience to Jesus Christ.
2 Corinthians 10:3-5

AFFIRMATION

I will no longer give a foothold to the enemy. My life is hidden in Christ.

WEEK 2

IDENTITY 101

Day 12 - 14

Take the time over the next few days to read through and pray these affirmations and scriptures from during the week. Don't forget to do the daily mind renewal plan.

SCRIPTURE PRAYERS

I thank You, Father that I do not walk as a natural man any longer but I am a spirit and a child of the Highest. I can hear your truths and judge righteously. The natural man cannot know the mind of the Lord but my old man is dead, and I have the mind of Christ. I can understand all your ways. In Jesus' name, Amen

Father, I thank you for the revelation that for although I live in the natural realm, I don't wage a military campaign employing human weapons, using manipulation to achieve my aims. Instead, my spiritual weapons are energized with divine power to dismantle strongholds effectively. I can demolish every deceptive imagination that opposes God and breaks through every arrogant attitude that is raised in defiance of Your true knowledge. I capture, like prisoners of war, every thought and insist that it bow in obedience to Jesus Christ.

Father, I cast off the old sinful nature, which was never your will for me anyway. I do not belong to this world any longer; I am a citizen of heaven. I am led by the Holy Spirit and have set aside all jealousy and quarrelsome attitudes. I have learned to walk in your spirit and have found maturity in Christ.

Thank you, Jesus that I have the mind of Christ, thank you that You have given me this gift. I can now think like you and talk like you and live the way You want me to live. Reveal to me what area you want me to work on over this study. I commit this time solely and entirely to You and trust that I can experience a breakthrough in this area. You are my faithful God; there is none like you.

AFFIRMATIONS

I am the temple of the Living God, and You take delight in me and who I am. It is your enjoyment to commune with me.

I shall not be known after the flesh but my Spirit. I refer to my spirit and not my efforts, abilities nor circumstances.

It is no longer I who lives but Christ who lives in me. I have the mind of Christ and will walk in righteousness before my God.

I will no longer give a foothold to the enemy. My life is hidden in Christ.

WEEK THREE
LIVING WORD 101

Week Three Daily Plan (Days 15-21)

This week, we will be tackling the "mountains" in our individual lives. A mountain is any obstacle to be removed as you seek to walk in spiritual victory. Choose an area in which you will continue to renew your mind for the remainder of this study. If you do not know what that is, take some time today to pray and ask the Lord what area He wants you to focus on.

Quiet Time with the Lord

- Make sure you have your usual time with the Lord daily

Bible Study

- Read days 15-17 and complete the Bible study questions
- Days 18-21 Speak all the daily affirmations & scripture prayers

Renewing the Mind Daily Plan

- Continue the below mind renewal plan daily

Renewing the Mind Daily Suggestions

- Before you start, gather any materials or printables you are going to need

- Before you start mind renewal each day take a few moments in thanksgiving for what God is going to do in you as you renew your mind.

- At the end of each mind renewal session write down any revelations you received from the Lord in your personal journal or the mind renewal weekly tracker.

- Set the alarm for a minimum of 7 times a day ideally every hour and have armed with you scriptures that you are going to meditate on. You can also do your faith actions in these times.

- Before you go to bed take a scripture and meditate on this and see yourself in that scripture.

Renewing the Mind Daily Plan – Week Three

***Day 15** We are going to practice prayer reading. Find 3-5 scriptures or a portion in the Bible that addresses your particular mountain and follow the steps in Day 15 on prayer reading. (You can also find some relevant scriptures in the appendix)

***Day 16** Let's renew our mind using scripture prayers. Take the scriptures you wrote on Day 15 and follow the How to steps on day 16 on scripture prayers in the study.

***Day 17** We are going to practice scripture journaling today. Please follow the steps on day 17 of the study.

***Day 18-21** Take all the truths in your journal & scripture prayers you received this week and meditate on these in your mind renewal time. Feel free to use more of the tools we learn this week

Faith Actions

- What action of faith is the Lord asking you to do today? This could be praying a scripture prayer or speaking out some affirmations.
- Do your faith action 7 times a day.

WEEK 3

LIVING WORD 101

Day 15

PRAYER – READING

It is funny really. I spent many years believing and being taught that I had to read at least seven chapters of the bible every day to truly understand the Word and grow in Christ. Don't get me wrong; reading the word is fantastic and one of the greatest gifts to christians given by God. Prayer reading is a great way to take time and indeed muse over the word. Muse is one of the definitions used in Hebrew translations of meditating.

The definition of 'muse' is "to think about something carefully and for a long time.
Synonyms: contemplate, meditate, ponder, reflect, ruminate and speculate

So when we take the word of God and take our time to have a conversation with the Lord not only are we proactively taking careful consideration as we go through the Word, fully digesting it and being sensitive; We are making it a time to commune with God with our whole heart and mind. No longer should we merely read the Bible religiously as something we must do out of compulsion, but it can be a precious opportunity to grow even closer to Him.

It is not enough to study the Bible – we must talk to God as we study. Bible study is meant to lead us to a conversation with God by giving u the "conversational material" for our prayer life. It provides the language we use as we talk to Him. Using the Bible and speaking the Word back to God makes prayer easy and enjoyable. It turns "up the volume" in our conversation with God – Mike Bickle

The Benefits of Prayer - Reading

1 – Helps Renew our minds

2 - Hearing from the Lord and His will on those scriptures

3 - We are proactively declaring the truth of the word

4 - We are standing in agreement with that word.

THERE ARE 2 MAIN TYPES OF SCRIPTURE:

1 - Scriptures that declare a thing/command/ to obey

2 - Scriptures that we stand in faith to believe

Here is an example of prayer reading.

1 Corinthians 13:13

And now abide faith, hope, love, these three; but the greatest of these is love

Step 1 – Read slowly

I would read the scripture very slowly and try to be actively still on the inside while listening to the Lord.

Step 2 – Acknowledge the type of scripture

You can see here that we would stand in agreement/faith with this scripture.

Step 3 – Ask the Holy Spirit for revelation & pray

I would ask Holy Spirit "what do you say about this word – show me how I can agree with you on this word" Then I would pray "Lord I commit to abiding in faith, hope and most of all, love. Lord show me today how I can show love in this area of my life" It's a simple prayer but what is prayer? It is a conversation with God.

An example of pray-reading a scripture to obey.

Philippians 2:3

³ Let nothing be done through selfish ambition or conceit, but in lowliness of mind let each esteem others better than himself.

Okay, this is something the Lord is telling us to do.

Next, I would commit my time to read over this scripture, word for word slowly.

My prayer would be

"Lord show me where I have acted in selfish ambition or conceit." Pause and wait. "I repent for any time I have not walked in lowliness of mind. I commit to not walking in pride. Lord, right now I commit my heart, and I renew my mind to this truth, that I must esteem others better than myself. Holy Spirit I need your help, I receive your help now, in Jesus' name".

And that is prayer reading. It is having a conversation with the Lord on each scripture and committing to live it out. You could easily do one scripture a day.

SCRIPTURE PRAYER

Father, thank you for giving me the living Word of God, which is full of living power, like a two-edged sword. It penetrates to the very core of my being where my soul, spirit, bone, and marrow meet! It interprets and reveals my real thoughts and secret motives of my heart."
Hebrews 4:12

AFFIRMATION

The truth of your Word and peace flows through my whole being like a river. And every area of my life is richly nourished by the sustenance of peace that comes from that river.

BIBLE STUDY QUESTIONS

➤ How does the Bible tell us we should muse on the Word?

➤ Do you think God wants you to muse on Scripture? If so, how can you commit to that today?

➤ Choose an area where you need to come into agreement with God, and talk to Him about it. What did you observe?

WEEK 3

LIVING WORD 101

Day 16

SCRIPTURE PRAYERS

I learned about scripture prayers about 2 or 3 years ago it has been a favorite tool I use to renew my mind to bring my focus onto the Lord and also to ensure that I am praying according to God's will.

Today we are going to focus on taking scripture and writing prayers that we can pray daily. Now a simple way you could do this is to take the prayers you said to the Lord in your prayer-reading time, write them down and pray them over your area of renewal every day. But I also like utilizing resources that already have scripture prayers like I have added in the appendix for you to utilise fully. But I also believe there is nothing quite as powerful as writing your own, based on scripture and inspired by your own personal time with the Lord.

In both the OT and NT scripture prayers were used. An example In the NT was when Peter and John were released in Acts 4 the church responded in prayer quoting Psalm 2:1-2.

Acts 4:24-26
24 So when they heard that, they raised their voice to God with one accord and said: "Lord, You are God, who made heaven and earth and the sea, and all that is in them, 25 who [a]by the mouth of Your servant David have said:

'Why did the nations rage,
And the people plot vain things?
26 The kings of the earth took their stand,
And the rulers were gathered together
Against the LORD and against His Christ.'

When we are meditating and learning about the scriptures, these are powerful tools we can use in the process of creating scripture prayers. This can enable us to know exactly that when we are declaring something over our lives, or agreeing with scripture we are making scripturally informed requests using real truths from the

Word and not our desires or worldly influences. We are taking off the lies of this world and the opinions of our flesh, and we are putting on truth. The truth will set us free from chains and bondages, bad habits and emotions; it helps us stay focused on Him when we would otherwise prefer to keep our mind on the earthly matters and concerns.

STEPS TO WRITING OUR SCRIPTURE PRAYERS

Below is an example of writing a scripture prayer.

For me, I have experienced deep wounds and pain from rejection from friends and family. We all know that when we stand for Christ there sometimes can be people who don't agree with our new way of life. Or let's be honest, we hurt someone, and they hurt us back. Either way, I cannot tell you how much writing scripture has helped me on the path of forgiveness.

Step one – Find a scripture that is relevant to the toxic thought you are trying to renew your mind about.

A excellent scripture for forgiveness is:

Colossians 3:13-14
[13] bearing with one another, and forgiving one another if anyone has a complaint against another; even as Christ forgave you, so you also must do. [14] But above all these things put on love, which is the bond of perfection.

Step two – Take the time to pray and ask the Holy Spirit to show us how we can apply this scripture to our lives.

Step three - Once you have prayed, you are going to write this out in your own words coupled with what truths God placed on your heart. Here is mine:

Lord, I thank you that you call me to take joy in your word and I want to be obedient with your word so today I commit to bearing with my sister/brother, and I willingly forgive them, not in my strength but by your might. I thank you that I have been forgiven and now you call me to forgive them. At all times and by your grace I will put on and wrap myself in unselfish love towards them, that is the bridge that brings unity, and I know that this is the perfect way to bring unity when I seek the best for them.

Thank you, Jesus, In your name I pray, Amen.

Step 4 – Faith Action

There are many ways of what you could do with these scripture prayers. You could turn them into short affirmations, put them on your wall, and set your alarm to meditate on this prayer and corresponding scripture several times a day. In my example, the Lord has to lead me to act on the scripture and give a peace offering to this friend. Whichever you choose to ensure that you put this into action as faith without works is dead.

Assignment

So today take scripture and have a practice at writing out a scripture prayer. Write one below:

If you are struggling with scripture to help you, I love the website www.openbible.info. You type in the search box the topic you are looking for scripture on and it lists back to you the top scriptures voted by other believers that they have found most useful. When I type in 'forgiveness' there are over 100 scriptures! Praise the Lord.

BIBLE STUDY QUESTIONS

➢ Why do you think Peter and John spoke using scripture prayers? (Acts 4:24:6)

➢ By using scripture prayers do you think it can unlock a deeper understanding of Gods will? If yes how?

➢ How do you believe utilizing scripture prayers is an effective way to renew the mind?

SCRIPTURE PRAYER

Father, I long for more revelation of your truth, for I love the light of your word as I meditate on your decrees. In the middle of the night, I awake to give thanks to you because of all your revelations; it is so right and true! Day and night your Words are always on my lips, Your words fill my life with prosperity and success and I am forever thankful!

Psalms 119:48, 62 Joshua 1:8

AFFIRMATION

Today I walk in the fear the LORD and serve him faithfully with all my heart. I will meditate and consider what great things He has done for me.

WEEK 3

LIVING WORD 101

Day 17

SCRIPTURE JOURNALING

How are you today? I am praying for you that you are starting to understand the power and authority that has been given to us through the Word of God to renew our minds.

Today we are going to look at scripture journaling. Scripture journaling is a practical way to take off the old lies and put on truth. It is also a great tool to use for scripture prayers. When I get to the end of a scripture journaling session I have received such wisdom that I can take the truths and turn them into prayers and utilize this throughout an area I am trying to address (and use them also as affirmations, more on this later).

There are many types of journaling, but I like utilizing the scripture as a primary way to determine whether the thoughts I am having are genuinely lined up with the Lords. Renewing the mind is meant to help line us up perfectly with the mind of Christ, and so this is why I love using His scripture.

We are meant to take EVERY thought captive to the obedience of Christ.

Scripture journaling is one of the tools that I love to use and have seen some of the most significant turn arounds for me, whether it is addressing anger, unforgiveness, anxiety, loss of a loved one, fear, or doubt. No matter what it is, if utilized properly this method coupled with God's Word is going to bring about transformation.

With scripture journaling we are going to take a mountain that we are struggling with and deal with it using this method. In the Appendix is a link to a scripture journaling form that you can use for this exercise.

Steps for Scripture Journaling

1. I write down the thoughts that I have been circulating inside my mind. If I am going through a trial at the time, often they can be negative. I like to put numbers next to each thought. But as I am growing in mind renewal and walking day by day in the mind of Christ, I like to have a little page to the side where I write down points the Lord shows me to be grateful for even in this trial. The bible says to count it all as joy when we fall into various temptations, so that is what I like to do by capturing those thoughts. I remind you that it says take EVERY thought captive, so take them all!

2. Once I have written them down I identify what the main topic is procrastination, doubt, unbelief, etc. I then look up the scriptures again relevant to that mountain, and I write out the scripture.

3. I then write a scripture prayer or biblical affirmation about that particular thought. Sometimes the scriptures relate to more than one thought, and so I number the scriptures in correspondence to those additional thoughts.

4. What I have sometimes done is to then put the whole document on my wall or my phone, and I would meditate on the truths throughout the day or many more days if need be until my mind was changed on this area. Being led by the Lord, I would then delete the lies which have been taken captive and only keep the truths to meditate on.

I have learned over the years that our thoughts and words have power and I choose to meditate on the truth of the word of God. It is powerful enough within itself to transform me. A double-edged sword has sharp edges on both sides and can cut in 2 directions. It separates the truth from the lie in the quickest manner.

Hebrews 4:12
12 For the word of God is living and powerful, and sharper than any two-edged sword, piercing even to the division of soul and spirit, and of joints and marrow, and is a discerner of the thoughts and intents of the heart.

How often is this necessary?

I get often asked "Well this scripture journaling seems like it is a long process! How often and when should I do this?" For me when I am dealing with a challenging trial or if I sense that this is a very difficult area that is causing me much distress I would be scripture journaling the initial time and taking those truths and using them to renew my mind several times a day (more on that later). If more thoughts come up, I add them to the scripture journal and keep adding the truth to it and then utilizing it to renew my mind (especially if I have crossed a line in disobedience). Every time my flesh walks in disobedience, it's time to apply the truth again and again as we have to be ready to punish every area of disobedience our flesh is walking in.

2 Corinthians 10:5-6
5 casting down arguments and every high thing that exalts itself against the knowledge of God, bringing every thought into captivity to the obedience of Christ, 6 and being ready to punish all disobedience when your obedience is fulfilled.

ASSIGNMENT

Today we are going to practice scripture journaling. What toxic thoughts have you been facing lately that you are struggling with? Let's take this time to scripture journal.

BIBLE STUDY QUESTIONS

➢ Why is it important to take off lies and put on truths?

➢ How is scripture the most effective way to do this?

➢ Do you think logic or our opinions are the best way to take off lies and put on truth? If not why?

➢ When do you think is the best time to utilize scripture journaling?

➢ Hebrews 4:12 speaks of the Word judging our innermost thoughts. Why is the word so powerful?

➢ Pray and ask the Lord to show you which area (or areas) you need to focus on today to renew your mind.

SCRIPTURE PRAYER

Lord, I commit to you to be an example for all to see of your faithfulness and truth living through my life. May authentic love be my banner as I diligently remain in your word meditating and devouring Your truths and teaching them to others. 1 Timothy 4:11-14

AFFIRMATION

I am partnering with the Holy Spirit who is doing a deep inner working in me. I will bless the Lord who has counseled me; indeed, my heart (mind) instructs me in the night.

WEEK 3

LIVING WORD 101

Day 18-21

Take the time over the next few days to read through and pray these affirmations and scriptures from during the week. Don't forget to do the daily mind renewal plan

SCRIPTURE PRAYERS

Father, thank you for giving me the living Word of God, which is full of living power, like a two-edged sword. It penetrates to the very core of my being where my soul, spirit, bone, and marrow meet! It interprets and reveals my exact thoughts and secret motives of my heart."

Father, I long for more revelation of your truth, for I love the light of your word as I meditate on your decrees. In the middle of the night, I awake to give thanks to you because of all your revelations; it is so right and true! Day and night your Words are always on my lips, Your words fill my life with prosperity and success and I am forever thankful!

Lord, I commit to you to be an example for all to see of your faithfulness and truth living through my life. May authentic love be my banner as I diligently remain in your word meditating and devouring Your truths and teaching them to others.

AFFIRMATIONS

The truth of your Word and peace flows through my whole being like a river. And every area of my life is richly nourished by the sustenance of peace that comes from that river.

Today I walk in the fear of the LORD and serve him faithfully with all my heart. I will meditate and consider what great things He has done for me.

I am partnering with the Holy Spirit who is doing a deep inner working in me. I will bless the Lord who has counseled me; indeed, my heart (mind) instructs me in the night.

WEEK FOUR
BIBLICAL AFFIRMATIONS 101

Week Four Daily Plan (Days 22-28)

This week and the remainder of the study we will be tackling Mountains. Congratulations as you have now completed 21 days of renewing of the mind and you should be starting to see some changes in your thinking and behavior. Don't stop now; we need to keep going.

Quiet Time with the Lord

- Make sure you have your usual time with the Lord daily

Bible Study

- Read days 22-26 and complete the Bible study questions
- Days 27-28 Speak all the daily affirmations & scripture prayers

Renewing the Mind Daily Plan

- Continue the below mind renewal plan daily

Renewing the Mind Daily Suggestions

- Before you start, gather any materials or printables you are going to need

- Before you start mind renewal each day take a few moments in thanksgiving for what God is going to do in you as you renew your mind.

- At the end of each mind renewal session write down any revelations you received from the Lord in your personal journal or the mind renewal weekly tracker.

- Set the alarm for a minimum of 7 times a day ideally every hour and have armed with you scriptures that you are going to meditate on. You can also do your faith actions in these times.

- Before you go to bed take a scripture and meditate on this and see yourself in that scripture.

Renewing the Mind Daily Plan – Week Four

*__Day 24__ Today we are going to take the F.E.L.L.O.W.S.H.I.P prayers in the back of this book and start speaking these truths to yourself.

*__Day 25__ Today I want you to take some time to journal. Journal what your life is going to be like when this mountain is removed from your life. Praise God in expectation

*__Day 26__ Pick 2 key scriptures that you have been using to renew your mind with this week and practice repeating and emphasizing each word. Remember to be slow and intentional.

*__Day 27- 28__ Take all the truths in your journal & scripture prayers you received this week and meditate on these in your mind renewal time. You can also repeat any of the above tasks today.

Faith Actions
- What action of faith is the Lord asking you to do today? This could be, declaring your scripture cards, mirror exercise or praying the scripture prayers.
- Do your faith action 7 times a day.

WEEK 4

BIBLICAL AFFIRMATIONS 101

Day 22

BIBLICAL AFFIRMATION

We have to give much time to speak the truth from Gods Word. For instance, when you are trying to heal your body, you have to take out the harmful foods or practices that could be making you sick. But you also have to take the time to feed your body with the nourishing foods, supplements, and exercises that are going to build you back up again. Likewise, we are taking off the lies that so easily beset us and feeding our souls with the rich nourishment of the Word of God.

What we mean by affirmations is speaking out loud the Word of God in a personalised way. Who does the word say you are? What does the word say you can do? We take all these truths and take it word for word/in your words based on scripture and speak these out loud daily. I need to emphasize that when we are engaging in biblical affirmations, it must be done solely based on biblical truths and not just what we want to happen.

Proverbs 18:20-21

A man's belly shall be satisfied with the fruit of his mouth; and with the increase of his lips shall he be filled. Death and life are in the power of the tongue: and they that love it shall eat the fruit thereof.

Many of us have spent years speaking over and over again the words of this world, and we have also spent many years eating the fruit (albeit fruit that rots) that have been born out of that place. Are you ready to bear fruit that lives forever which nourishes the type of life that God has stored and prepared for us?

For example, if you are struggling with your relationship with your friend, for most people, the initial thought & speech is "I can't stand that person, they have hurt me too much and I cannot forgive. I need just to move on," but the truth is in God's Word.

Matthew 6:15
But if you do not forgive others their trespasses, neither will your Father forgive your trespasses.

Luke 6:27
But I say to you who hear, Love your enemies, do good to those who hate you.

So my biblical affirmation would then be: "I will forgive my sister, I love her with my heart. I will bless my sister and not speak negatively about her. I will love her with the love of Christ."

But isn't this lying? No. There is a stark difference between lying and speaking in faith according to God's word instead of the circumstances we find ourselves in. Paul said it brilliantly:

2 Corinthians 4:13
Since we have the same spirit of faith, according to what is written, "I believed, and therefore I spoke" we also believe, and therefore we speak.

But I would like to add a disclaimer. It says I "BELIEVED" it is not enough to wish and hope that these biblical affirmations and scriptures are true we have to believe and act in faith that the Lord's word is the final authority.

Hebrews 11:6

"But without faith, it is impossible to please Him, for he who comes to God must believe that He is a rewarder of those who diligently seek Him."

Dear friend as you do biblical affirmations, please engage our almighty God and seek Him in His beautiful truths.

Biblical Affirmation Cards

We can write the scriptures out in an affirmation style from what we receive in our scripture journaling exercises or even scripture prayers. I love writing these out on cards like 4x3 filing cards or have them printed out on paper and posted around the house.

When we take the time to speak these throughout the day, they are emphasizing core truths and actively renewing our mind. Repetition and focus are vital and essential to let the words soak into our hearts and bring about transformation.

Assignment

Have a try at writing some affirmation cards or even printing the affirmations from this week or in the appendix and put them around your home. Also try having some affirmations on your mirror.

Mirror Exercise

Knowing who I am in Christ has been life transforming, and I love taking these truths of who I am (which you can find in the appendix) and placing them on my mirrors at home.

Assignment

Take the time to print these and every time you look at yourself in the mirror speak these beautiful truths.

SCRIPTURE PRAYER

His covenant of peace shall not be removed: The Lord who has mercy on me has promised that even if the mountains should depart, and the hills are removed His loving kindness yet shall not depart from me neither shall His covenant of peace be removed. Isaiah 54:10

AFFIRMATION

I am profoundly rooted and secure in God's love

WEEK 4

BIBLICAL AFFIRMATIONS 101

Day 23

JOURNALING

Journaling is one of my favorite activities I love having a pen and paper near when I am in silence before God and listening to what He has to say to me. In these beautiful moments, I love to capture and repeat back to myself over and over again His truths. I used to have these written on random pieces of paper until the Lord convicted me about this. He taught me to treasure the words He has spoken to me. So now I keep them in a centralized online journal.

Journaling is a powerful tool that I and many more use to document our daily life. We must practice to write down and keep a record of what we hear from the Lord.

Habakkuk 2:1-2

I will stand at my guard post
And station myself on the tower;
And I will keep watch to see what He will say to me,
And what answer I will give [as His spokesman] when I am reproved.

Then the Lord answered me and said,
"Write the vision
And engrave it plainly on [clay] tablets
So that the one who reads it will run.

This verse states that we must wait and see what the Lord is doing and write it down and make it plain. We have to practice seeing and hearing what God is saying to us, as we ask Holy Spirit for insight.

We are meant to be renewed in the Spirit of our mind. God holds a place in our minds, and He enables us to see through ideas, imaginations and godly thoughts. We must train ourselves to be sensitive to when the Lord is speaking to us. But the most important thing to remember is that our senses are not separate from the mind and we can use all our faculties to understand God's will for us. However, you receive from God write them down.

SCRIPTURE PRAYER

Father, I will stand at my guard post and station myself on the tower; and I will keep watch to see what You will say to me, and what answer I will give as Your spokesman when I am reproved. I will follow your commands and write the vision plainly So that anyone who reads it will be able to run with it. Habakkuk 2:1-2

AFFIRMATION

I am of great worth! Not forgotten/forsaken and in right standing with God.

WEEK 4

BIBLICAL AFFIRMATIONS 101

Day 24

F-E-L-L-O-W-S-H-I-P

I learned this acronym from Mike Bickle. These represent prayers that we can do to strengthen our inner man. These are a guide - only and its key to be led by the Spirit when praying. The acronym stands for ten prayer requests we can pray for ourselves, people, nations and strategic issues that face our world. Mike Bickle's copyright is the "right to copy", so I am so happy to include a short description here and in the appendix is a fuller copy of prayer guidance. For a fuller understanding, Mike Bickle has a free copy of this e-book on his website mikebickle.org

SUMMARY

F — Fear of God: Father, release the spirit of the fear of God into my heart (Ps. 86:11).

E — Endurance: Strengthen my spirit with endurance to do Your will (Col. 1:11).

L — Love: Father, pour out Your love in my heart in a greater measure (Phil. 1:9).

L — Light of glory: Father, let me see more of the light of Your glory (Acts 22:6–11; Ex. 33:18; Ps. 4:6).

O — One thing: I set my heart to be a "person of one thing" who regularly sits before You (Ps. 27:4).

W — Count me worthy: Strengthen me to have a worthy response to You in my life (2 Thessalonians. 1:11).

S — Speech: Set a guard over my lips that I may walk free from unclean speech (Eph. 4:29; Ps. 141:3).

H — Humility: Jesus, I want to learn from You how to walk with a lowly heart (Mt. 11:29).

I — Insight (wisdom): Give me insight into Your Word, will, and ways (Col. 1:9–10).

P — Peace and joy: Strengthen my heart with peace and joy that overpower fear (Phil. 4:7).

SCRIPTURE PRAYER

I thank you, Lord that as I meditate on your word that my soul prospers and this means that every area of my life will prosper as I stay focused on You and your precious truths. My heart is full of thanksgiving.

3 John 1:2

AFFIRMATION

God is my stronghold. I am never alone and never forsaken.

BIBLE STUDY QUESTIONS

➢ Why is it important when using affirmation cards to have them focus on biblical truths?

➢ What words have you spoken about your mountain that could have had a negative impact?

➤ What are three truths you can think of now that would counteract the negative words/thoughts?

➤ Hebrews 11:6 Why is it impossible to please God without faith?

➤ This week we are focusing on putting on truth. What would your life look like after 63 days putting on truths?

BIBLICAL AFFIRMATIONS 101

Day 25

REPEATING AND EMPHASISING SCRIPTURE

Repetition is so important when it comes to renewing the mind. Many times I have been renewing my mind regularly over and over on the same area as a tool to get my mind in line with the Lord's. The great thing is that I have seen so many breakthroughs in my life in particular with some challenging areas such as fear, anxiety and food addiction.

One of the key ways that I have seen works wonderfully is with the spoken repetition and slow meditation on scripture word for word. I liken it to "chewing" on the word of God. Chewing on the word is like chewing food; digestion starts in the process of chewing first before it enters the stomach. It also is the same with the word when we take the time to slowly and repeatedly meditate on it; our brain, heart and the power of the Holy Spirit work together allowing the truth to go deeper.

Jeremiah 15:16

Thy words were found, and I did eat them; and thy word was unto me the joy and rejoicing of mine heart: for I am called by thy name, O LORD God of hosts.

Psalm 119:103
How sweet are Your words to my taste, sweeter than honey in my mouth?

MATTHEW 4:4

"But Jesus replied, It is written and forever remains written,

'Man shall not live by bread alone, but by every word that proceeds from the mouth of God.'"

The precious word of God has been given to us for our nourishment we need it to sink deep into our most inner being. The word is life for our soul and strength to our body. So we want to treasure it for the gift that it is and take the time to feed on this word slowly.

One of the definitions of meditation in the Bible is to 'muse'. This means, to consider deeply and repeatedly. The goal is not to necessarily memorize the scripture alone, but to draw out all the goodness possible from that very word and let it wash over us and cleanse us from the inside out.

How can we take this and put it into practice daily? Let's practice repeating and emphasizing the scriptures.

For instance, if I am trying to renew my mind to the scripture:

Be quick to listen, be slow to speak and be slow to become angry.

Step one: I would take the above scripture and slowly emphasize each word. And repeat this as many times as there are words in the scripture.

Step two: So this scripture has 14 words in that verse, so I would say the scripture 14 times emphasizing the next word each time I read it.

Step three: I would then say a prayer back to the Lord asking for revelation or guidance.

ASSIGNMENT

For some, this can be a difficult concept to understand in written form. So I have recorded a short example based on the above scripture for a clear understanding. This clip can is found on Sound Cloud. Here is the link: https://soundcloud.com/user-535341093/week-4-repeating-emphasing Take the time to listen to that recording and have a practice yourself.

It is fascinating how we may never have seen how some keywords within that scripture give us a different perspective. Praise God for the revelation of God's word.

Muse & Pause

Another way I like to do this is through taking a few words at a time and pausing, musing and talking back to myself like I am describing the scripture to someone else and also do a bit of scripture prayer at the end. In the Hebraic meanings of meditating many of them refer to speaking to oneself or to 'Ponder' (meaning to converse with oneself). Talking to ourselves is one of the main principles of affirmations. Doing this over and over again brings excellent revelation. Below is an example.

Be Quick To Listen

"Okay Sophia, I have to be truly quick to listen, that means listening quickly, this means being sharp and paying attention, okay when it is time to listen, I can't be distracted and multi-task, God truly wants me to give full attention when listening to. I will be quick to listen."

Be Slow To Speak

Okay, Sophia, this is a command. This is something I must do. That means I can't be speaking slowly and interrupting someone at the same time. I can't be trying to get my words in wherever possible. I need to choose my words carefully. God, help me to speak my words slowly.

SCRIPTURE PRAYER

Father, I found Your words, and I ate them, and your words became to me a joy and the delight of my heart, for I am called by your name, O Lord, God of hosts. And I have discovered that bread alone will not satisfy, but true life is found in every word, which continually goes forth from Your mouth. How sweet are your living promises to me; more delicious than honey is your revelation.

AFFIRMATION

I have a God centered mind, and I have a sound and stable mind being renewed daily.
Jeremiah 15:16, Matthew 4:4, Psalms 119:103

WEEK 4

BIBLICAL AFFIRMATIONS 101

Day 26

VAIN REPETITIONS

It is essential and necessary to address the scripture about vain repetitions.

"When ye pray, use not vain repetitions, as the heathen do: for they think that they shall be heard for their much speaking" Matthew 6:7, KJV

In the Sermon on the Mount Jesus noted that we must not make vain repetitions in prayer. Having repetition is fine but NOT vain ones. Using vain repetitions is when we take words that don't have meaning or are useless. Well, firstly the word of God is not useless; it is stronger and sharper than any two-edged sword. However, we must be mindful not to let our renewing the mind sessions be done just for the sake of them. You have to take the time to indeed ensure you mean what you say and believe the words of God to be strong and mighty in the pulling down of strongholds.

The Holy Spirit taught me that often we have learned lots of quips from the Christian culture and say things when situations come up that are in line with the word but often they are vain repetitions spoken without faith. Such as "I rebuke that in Jesus name," "I plead the blood of Jesus," "I am blessed and highly favored", "The devil is a liar," These are all true and fine to speak IF we truly believe. But if we are just saying them for the sake of it, then they are vain and create a false belief of a renewed mind.

BIBLE STUDY QUESTIONS

➤ What image comes up in your mind when you think of chewing on the word?

- Jeremiah 15:16, Psalm 119:103 and Matthew 4 Talks about eating the Word or refers food to the Word. Why? What are the benefits of viewing and meditating on the word like this?

- Talking to ourselves can be a bit funny. But the Bible teaches us to ponder on the word. Let's practice. Take Matthew 4:4 and write down below what you discover as you ponder on the word.

- Repetition is essential but how can we avoid vain repetitions?

SCRIPTURE PRAYER

My wonderful Father, I receive the teachings of Jesus Christ as truth to me. Holy Spirit, help me to put off everything that is of the old un-renewed self. I receive your power, person, and guidance into my mind, to govern my mind, direct my mind, and change every spiritual foundation that my mind is connected to and make it your foundation. Holy Spirit I choose to give you full control so that I can put on the new self entirely, my heavenly self. I thank you that my renewed self looks like your image, thinks like Jesus and is righteous and holy.

AFFIRMATION

Lord, I thank you for the faith You have given me, and as I renew my mind, I will watch unbelief disappear day by day.

WEEK 4

BIBLICAL AFFIRMATIONS 101

Day 27-28

Take the time over the next few days to read through and pray these affirmations and scriptures from during the week. Don't forget to do the daily mind renewal plan.

SCRIPTURE PRAYERS

His covenant of peace shall not be removed: The Lord who has mercy on me has promised that even if the mountains should depart, and the hills are removed His loving kindness yet shall not depart from me neither shall His covenant of peace be removed. Father, I will stand at my guard post And station myself on the tower; And I will keep watch to see what You will say to me, And what answer I will give as Your spokesman when I am reproved. I will follow your commands and write the vision plainly So that anyone who reads it will be able to run with it.

I thank you, Lord that as I meditate on your word that my soul prospers and this means that in every area of my life will thrive as I stay focused on You and your precious truths. My heart is full of thanksgiving.

Father, I found Your words, and I ate them, and your words became to me a joy and the delight of my heart, for I am called by your name, O Lord, God of hosts. And I have discovered that bread alone will not satisfy, but true life is found in every word, which continually goes forth from Your mouth. How sweet are your living promises to me; more delicious than honey is your revelation.

My wonderful Father, I receive the teachings of Jesus Christ as truth to me. Holy Spirit, help me to put off everything that is of the old un-renewed self. I receive your power, person, and guidance into my mind, to govern my mind, direct my mind, and change every spiritual foundation that my mind is connected to and make it your foundation. Holy Spirit I choose to give you full control so that I can put on the new self fully, my heavenly self. I thank you that my renewed self looks like your image, thinks like Jesus and is righteous and holy.

AFFIRMATIONS

I am deeply rooted and secure in God's love

Lord, I thank you for the faith You have given me, and as I renew my mind, I watch unbelief disappear day by day.

I have a God centered mind, and I have a sound and stable mind being renewed daily.

God is my stronghold. I am never alone and never forsaken.

I am of great worth! Not forgotten/forsaken and in right standing with God.

WEEK FIVE

THOUGHT LIFE 101

Week Five Daily Plan (Days 29-35)

We are continuing with this journey. I am so excited for you and praying that you are being transformed daily. This week and next week we will be tackling our thought life and exchanging our thoughts for the thoughts of the mind of Christ. For the remainder of this study, let's add in 10 minutes before you sleep to meditate on the truths that God has revealed to you throughout the day.

Quiet Time with the Lord

- Make sure you have your usual time with the Lord daily

Bible Study

- Read days 29-31 and complete the Bible study questions
- Days 32-35 speak all the daily affirmations & scripture prayers

Renewing the Mind Daily Plan

- Continue the below mind renewal plan daily & 10 minutes review before you sleep.

Renewing the Mind Daily Suggestions

- Before you start, gather any materials or printables you are going to need

- Before you start mind renewal each day take a few moments in thanksgiving for what God is going to do in you as you renew your mind.

- At the end of each mind renewal session write down any revelations you received from the Lord in your personal journal or the mind renewal weekly tracker.

- Set the alarm for a minimum of 7 times a day ideally every hour and have armed with you scriptures that you are going to meditate on. You can also do your faith actions in these times.

- Before you go to bed take a scripture and meditate on this and see yourself in that scripture.

Renewing the Mind Daily Plan – Week Five

*Day 29 Today we are going to take some time and meditate on things above. Take the mountain you are demolishing and complete the Think On Model worksheet

*Day 30 Practice strengthening the God-given imagination the Lord has given you and practice the task on Day 30.

*Day 31 Today we are going to spend time talking to Holy Spirit about the mountain and the transformation so far and ask Him his views on the matter. Read day 31 to see the steps.

*Day 32- 35 Take all the truths in your journal & scripture prayers you received this week and meditate on these in your mind renewal time. You can also repeat any of the above tasks or from previous weeks on these days.

Faith Actions
- What action of faith is the Lord asking you to do today? This could be, declaring your scripture cards, mirror exercise or praying the scripture prayers.
- Do your faith action 7 times a day.

WEEK 5

THOUGHT LIFE 101

Day 29

THINK ON THESE THINGS

One of the great methods that the Lord showed me was to meditate on Philippians 4:8 as a way to renew my mind. By connecting it with a situation, event, or person and meditate on the truth concerning it. Paul told the Philippians to mentally dwell on and meditate on these truths continually and put them in their hearts. In the previous verses, we can see that this is used to enable us to overcome anything that leads us to become anxious or worried. The word teaches us to firstly give everything to God in prayer and much supplication, bringing all our requests to the Lord. This peace we receive that surpasses all understanding will then guard our hearts and minds.

He then goes on to tell us to walk out these truths seen in:

Philippians 4:8 (bold emphasis added)

8 Finally, brethren, whatever things are **true**, whatever things *are* **noble**, whatever things *are* **just**, whatever things *are* **pure**, whatever things *are* **lovely**, whatever things *are* of **good report**, if *there is* any **virtue** and if *there is* anything **praiseworthy**—meditate on these things. **9** The things which you learned and received and heard and saw in me, these do, and the God of peace will be with you.

We are going to breakdown these keywords highlighted in bold. The translation comes from the Greek translations in the Strong's Concordance.

- **True**

In Greek 'true' means whatever is worthy of credit, truthful and when tested it would, without doubt, prove this to be fact. It is something that cannot be hidden.

- **Noble/Venerable**

Honorable or dignified about a person or situation.

- **Just/Right**

Whatever is just, correct or right before the eyes of God, His standard of righteousness in His eyes about a thing or person.

- **Pure**

Whatever is pure, innocent, sacred, and perfect.

- **Lovely**

Whatever is pleasing, acceptable, agreeable and great. Only in Philippians 4:8 does it translate to anything that is worthy of having and embracing. Whatever is highly prized. It would also relate to a thing or quality in a person that you cherish.

- **Good Report/Admirable**

Something worthy of praise, or commendable about a person or thing.

- **Virtuous**

Any excellence of a person (in body or mind) or of a thing, an eminent endowment, property or quality, a good or gracious matter or act. Anything worthy of praise.

- **Praise Worthy**

Something that is worth enthusiastic acknowledgment in a way that promotes praise. Recognizing good in a person or situation.

- **Think on** (these things above)

Reckon (calculate, judge and conclude), reason, decide, think, meditate on. The Greek word *logízomai* is the root of the English terms "*logic, logical*" so we are going to reason to a logical decision on the above.

So how can we use this scripture to renew our minds on a situation, matter or person? I have created a method called the "Think On" model. In the appendix, is a form I have created for you!

STEPS TO USE THE 'THINK ON' MODEL

1. Write the topic you want to meditate on. Is it a person that has offended you? A situation that has happened, which has led you to fall into anger or dismay? Write this down.

2. Then we are going to pray and give this area to God and ask Him to show us the truth about this situation

3. Next, we are going to look at each area that the word tells us to meditate on and decide what is:
   TRUE – HONORABLE – RIGHT – PURE – LOVELY – ADMIRABLE – VIRTUOUS – PRAISEWORTHY

4. Once we have our list, we are going to write a statement for each, and we are going to take time in speaking these out as truths every day or several times a day until we have healing and peace about this situation. Let the peace of the Lord lead you.

*Note. Every time the situation comes up, you are going to meditate using the 'think on' statements.

Remember Paul went through great struggle and trial and great abundance also. Yet he was able to stay content in either situation. The key? Meditating on the truths that God has shown us through the word. Let's dig deeper together and meditate on these higher things.

BIBLE STUDY QUESTIONS

> ➢ Looking at the keywords to meditate on in Philippians 4:8 what is the opposite of these?

> ➢ How much time do you spend meditating on the negative?

> ➢ What is the benefit of "thinking on" the Philippians 4:8 truths in your life?

> ➢ Paul was able to be content in all circumstances. Why does meditating on the truth about a difficult situation help you stay content?

SCRIPTURE PRAYER

I have set the Lord continually before me; Because He is at my right hand, I will not be shaken. *Today I will focus and keep moving forward and upwards from glory to glory not looking back, not entertaining thoughts of mine or others that are contrary to Your promises. Father, I keep my thoughts continually fixed on all that is authentic and real, honorable and admirable, beautiful and respectful, pure and holy, merciful and kind. I fasten my thoughts on Your glorious work, praising You always.*
Philippians 4:8

AFFIRMATION

With a deep longing, I seek You today, and I require of You today. It is of vital necessity as I search for You with all my heart.

WEEK 5

THOUGHT LIFE 101

Day 30

VISUALIZATION/IMAGINATION

From a young age, before I even knew Christ, God used the power of vision to show me things that were to come, or to bring warnings. When I was 18, I was involved in a near fatal car accident where I had two fingers amputated on my left hand. However, not many people know that before this just the day before I had a dream from the Lord that I would lose these fingers I woke up from my sleep and the two fingers I would lose the next day were numb. I had a witness to this at the time, and so it goes down as a record for me that God speaks to us in dreams and visions, utilizing the power of our image centers in our minds, our imagination. This was the beginning of a wondrous adventure of sweet communion and revelation not just for me but also to help others.

God has given us a wonderful gift of imagination to enable us to see how He sees and what He wants us to see.

God created us all to understand in image form; this is the master creator's handprint in our lives. We were created in His image after all.

There is, of course, the counterfeit, a new age protocol of visualization; this is not what I am referring to and will have no part in such matters. However, seeing the truth of God's word in image form is powerful and life transforming. Humans think in pictures.

Jesus always taught with parables and stories that cause us to imagine the storyline and apply it to our everyday life. When I read the Parables of Talents I imagine the men and what they did with their talents, it is all part of the purpose of the parables.

Matthew 13:34

All these things Jesus spoke to the multitude in parables, and without a parable, He did not speak to them,

Acts 2:17

*17 'And it shall come to pass in the last days, says God,
That I will pour out of My Spirit on all flesh;
Your sons and your daughters shall prophesy,
Your young men shall see visions,
Your old men shall dream dreams.*

In both the OT and NT God uses our imagination and the eyes of our heart to communicate with us. He also wants us to use our imagination for His glory, not the terrible things our flesh or the world wants to use their imagery for. Unfortunately, because of the fall, many of our imaginations have been distorted in darkness. God wants to reclaim our minds entirely for His glory.

2 Corinthians 10:4-5

4 (For the weapons of our warfare are not carnal, but mighty through God to the pulling down of strong holds;

5 Casting down imaginations, and every high thing that exalteth itself against the knowledge of God, and bringing into captivity every thought to the obedience of Christ;

Take back those imaginations for Christ!

We must love God with all of our heart, mind, and strength and part of our mind's function is imagination, and so we give this over to God, to be renewed to see the way He wants us to see.

Imagination is one of the best ways to renew the mind. Every second we are awake our brain is recording pictures similar to a movie, or photographer, we are capturing millions of clips.

How to use our imagination for renewing the mind

One of the meanings for meditating in Strong's Exhaustive Concordance is to imagine (haw-gaw).

It is pretty simple really, one of the easiest ways to use the imagination is when you read or meditate on scripture to view yourself in that scripture. But I will give a step by step process below.

Pre-requisites

- The Holy Spirit must be the leader, and He will emphasize what to focus on.
- Remain dependant continually on Him.
- Test every spirit – everything you receive should and must line up with the word of God on all sides.
- This is not a 6 step plan to perfection – be led by the Spirit.
- Only meditate on God and His words
- Spend time learning & knowing how to hear Gods voice

Step one: Once you have taken the time to write down a verse on a piece of paper or card, meditate, memorize and mutter it back to yourself during the day. I keep my scriptures in my mobile phone set as alerts throughout the day or in a place within my home that I frequently would see them.

Step two: Spend some quiet time alone with the Lord; you could play some instrumental worship music if you like. I keep a notepad with me jotting down thoughts or things I hear God speaking to me.

Step three: Ask the Lord what He wants you to see in this scripture. Ask Holy Spirit what He thinks about this scripture?

Step four: Speak the scripture back to yourself and discuss the scripture. Imagine yourself in that scripture and ask the Lord to reveal His heart about this scripture

Step five: Continue to jot down any thoughts or images the Lord wants you to keep

Step six: Act! If you have to repent of something, then do so, if you need to renew your mind on this further, do this over an extended period or days and implement any relevant changes that are needful.

BIBLE STUDY QUESTIONS

➢ Read 2 Corinthians 10:4 what types of thoughts do we need to bring into captivity?

➢ Why does God use our imaginations?

➢ Set a timer for 2 minutes and be still before the Lord. Jot down any images or thoughts you had. Did they line up with the word of God?

➢ Talk to the Lord about these thoughts and ask Him to reveal to you His thoughts on this matter. Jot them down below

SCRIPTURE PRAYER

Father, I ask you to continue to pour out your Spirit on everybody and cause our sons and daughters to prophesy, and our young men to see visions, and the old men to experience Your dreams!

Acts 2:17

AFFIRMATION

I am running my race in faithfulness. Jesus Christ and the cloud of witnesses are surrounding me watching. I am running a race with Christ, so I strip off every unnecessary weight and sin.

WEEK 5

THOUGHT LIFE 101

Day 31

TALKING TO HOLY SPIRIT & THE 5 SENSES

John 14:26 Amplified Bible (AMP)
26 But the [a]Helper (Comforter, Advocate, Intercessor—Counselor, Strengthener, Standby), the Holy Spirit, whom the Father will send in My name [in My place, to represent Me and act on My behalf], He will teach you all things. And He will help you remember everything that I have told you.

Our faithful friend, helper, leader, and teacher, the Holy Spirit. Where would we be without Him? Jesus promised that He would send us our wondrous counselor to guide us and teach us all things.

Praise God for His mighty hand in the process of us walking in the mind of Christ.

Whatever issue we are facing we must take the thoughts captive to the obedience to Christ and then an additional tool we can use here, is asking the Holy Spirit His thoughts on this area. Having this conversation as a priority is important. For some, this may be a difficult concept to comprehend as we focus a lot on talking through our issues with friends, family or seeking counsel from other sources.

We have to get back to asking the great Helper for assistance.

As a married woman, I know that God has called me to be my beloved husband's helper. But you know, sometimes husbands don't fully recognize that God ordained us to take this position and they struggle. Well many people do not understand that they can turn to the One that Jesus said is our helper and teacher – He is waiting, ready and able to help.

Ask Holy Spirit what He thinks and journal – what God says not everyone else's opinion. We have to learn how to hear from the Holy Spirit.

So we are going to practice this by spending time with Him and learning from Holy Spirit.

STEPS

Step one: In your quiet time with the Lord or any other significant time of the day bring a focal point regarding the mountain that you are addressing and we are going to ask Holy Spirit some questions.

Step two: Ask the Holy Spirit

- What do you think?
- What do you see when you look at this?
- When you look at this situation what do you see?
- What would you speak about this?
- How do you feel about this and discern about this?

Step three: Next we are going to be in silence before Him, and we are going to journal what we receive.

Step four: Have a conversation back, clarify and ensure everything you think you received lines up with the Word of God.

Step five: Ask the Lord how He wants you to apply these truths to your life.

Bible Study Questions

➢ In John 14:26 List all the ways Holy Spirit is here to help you.

➢ One of the ways is that He is a comforter. I like to ask Holy Spirit to show me how He can be my comforter. Take all the ways you wrote above how Holy Spirit wants to help you and spend 5 minutes asking Him how these truths can be applied to your life.

➢ Read through Habbakuk 2:1
What are the key things or actions we are to do when taking the time to hear the voice of the Lord?

➢ We have to practice seeing and hearing what God is saying to us as we ask Holy Spirit for insight. Ask the Holy Spirit to show you how you can apply the above actions into your life.

SCRIPTURE PRAYER

Thank you, Jesus, that you helped people in the past and today to understand truths of your word through parables to ignite the visual side of mankind. I thank you that I can still today receive your revelations in image form. I commit my imagination for your glory and purposes to see in word pictures, visions, and dreams. Matthew 13:34

AFFIRMATION

I walk on water today, no capsizing, no head barely above the waters of my life, EVER!!!

WEEK 5

THOUGHT LIFE 101

Days 32-35

Take the time over the next few days to read through and pray these affirmations and scriptures from during the week. Don't forget to do the daily mind renewal plan in the AM & PM.

SCRIPTURE PRAYERS

Father, I thank you for the revelation that for although I live in the natural realm, I don't wage a military campaign employing human weapons, using manipulation to achieve my aims. Instead, my spiritual weapons are energized with divine power to dismantle the defences behind which people hide effectively. I can demolish every deceptive fantasy that opposes God and breaks through every arrogant attitude that is raised in defiance of Your true knowledge. I capture, like prisoners of war, every thought and insist that it bow in obedience to Jesus the Anointed One."

Thank you, Jesus, that you helped people in the past and today to understand truths of your word through parables to ignite the visual side of mankind. I thank you that I can still today receive your truths in image form. I commit my imagination for your glory and purposes to see in word pictures, visions, and dreams.

Father, I keep my thoughts continually fixed on all that is authentic and real, honorable and admirable, beautiful and respectful, pure and holy, merciful and kind. I fasten my thoughts on Your glorious work, praising You always.

Father, I ask you to continue to pour out your Spirit on everybody and cause our sons and daughters to prophesy, and our young men to see visions, and the old men to experience Your dreams!

AFFIRMATIONS

With a deep longing, I seek You today, and I require of You today. It is of vital necessity as I search for You with all my heart.

I am running my race in faithfulness. Jesus Christ and the cloud of witnesses are surrounding me watching. I am running a race with Christ, so I strip off every unnecessary weight and sin.

I walk on water today, no capsizing, no head barely above the waters of my life, EVER!!!

I have set the Lord continually before me; Because He is at my right hand, I will not be shaken.

Today I will focus and keep moving forward and upwards from glory to glory not looking back, not entertaining thoughts of mine or others that are contrary to Your promises.

WEEK SIX

CHRIST FOCUS 101

Week Six Daily Plan (Days 36-42)

We are now two thirds of the way through completing this study. This week we are going to be focusing on taking off lies and putting on truth, so we can line up with the mind of Christ.

Quiet Time with the Lord

- Make sure you have your usual time with the Lord daily

Bible Study

- Read days 36-39 and complete the Bible study questions
- Days 40-42 Speak all the daily affirmations & scripture prayers

Renewing the Mind Daily Plan

- Continue the below mind renewal plan daily & 10 minutes review before you sleep.

Renewing the Mind Daily Suggestions

- Before you start, gather any materials or printables you are going to need

- Before you start mind renewal each day take a few moments in thanksgiving for what God is going to do in you as you renew your mind.

- At the end of each mind renewal session write down any revelations you received from the Lord in your personal journal or the mind renewal weekly tracker.

- Set the alarm for a minimum of 7 times a day ideally every hour and have armed with you scriptures that you are going to meditate on. You can also do your faith actions in these times.

- Before you go to bed take a scripture and meditate on this and see yourself in that scripture.

Renewing the Mind Daily Plan – Week Six

*Day 36 Today we are going to practice meditating on God's Word again. Try talking to yourself about the scriptures and talk to Holy Spirit about the scriptures. You can also put your name in the appropriate places and speak them back to yourself. Choose scriptures that you have been leaning on over the past five weeks.

*Day 37 Practice strengthening the God-given imagination and practice the task on Day 30.

*Day 38 Today we are going to spend time being still and listening to what the Lord wants to say to you. Commit the last few weeks to Him and ask of Him what thoughts do you still need to deal with.

*Day 39 Let's spend some time taking thoughts captive and exchanging them for truth. Use the exercise from day 38

*Day 40- 42 Take all the truths in your journal & scripture prayers you received this week and meditate on these in your mind renewal time. You can also repeat any of the above tasks or from previous weeks on these days.

Faith Actions
- What action of faith is the Lord asking you to do today? This could be, declaring your scripture cards, mirror exercise or praying the scripture prayers.
- Do your faith action 7 times a day.

WEEK 6

CHRIST FOCUS 101

Day 36

MEDITATION

I remember the days when I used to hear people talk about meditation; I believed that this was for those who are Buddhists, Hindu or New Age individuals. But I realized through careful study of the Word that the practice of meditation originated from the Bible. There are so many scriptures on meditation that it is clear that this is part of God's plan to benefit us and bring us to a place of alignment with His thoughts.

Joshua 1:8

This Book of the Law shall not depart from your mouth, but you shall meditate on in it day and night that you may observe to do according to all that is written in it. For then you will make your way prosperous, and then you will have good success.

Meditating on God's word day and night through speaking and thinking His word continually, will lead us to observe to do His will.

Whatever decisions we make, happen because of:

1. A **thought** that turned into a...
2. **Word** and then became a...
3. **Deed**

This both works in the negative aspect and also in the positive, if we meditate on wrong and negative thoughts it's going to start dictating what we speak to be negative that will eventually lead to committing a negative deed.

But the same can be said for when we meditate on truth, the word of God WILL make our way prosperous. This is God's formula for our success.

3 John 1:2

Beloved, I wish above all things that thou mayest prosper and be in health, even as thy soul prospereth.

It is God's will that we prosper as our soul prospers. This scripture shows us that our soul can indeed prosper and grow. To prosper means to be blessed in that area of our life. By thinking, speaking and doing the word of God, this leads to great prosperity.

Meditation means to murmur, ponder, think, speak, to think deeply and focus.

HOW OFTEN & WHEN SHOULD WE BE MEDITATING?

This is often a question I get asked, so let's go to the word and have a look at some examples in the life of King David – a man after Gods own heart:

Psalm 1:1-3 David speaks of meditating on God's word day and night.

Psalm 63:1 David speaks here that 'EARLY' will he seek the Lord.

Psalm 63:6, 119:62 On His bed he meditates in the night watches.

Psalm 119:164 7 times a day shall I praise the Lord because of His righteous judgments.

WAYS TO MEDITATE

DAILY ALARMS

I love to set alarms in my phone daily seven times a day as a minimum to remind me to meditate on a particular scripture or set of scriptures that relate to an area that I need to renew my mind about. Take the time to stop regularly in your day, pause and meditate – it is such a healthy practice for the mind, despite our busy schedules. Stop and meditate on these scriptures. Soon you will not need to set an alarm as you would've trained yourself to stop and meditate throughout the day regularly.

COMMIT TO 21 DAYS

It takes 21 days to build a habit. Stopping for even 1 minute several times a day and applying the word of God for 21 days consistently has been proven to cause measurable transformation. Through this study, we are completing three rounds of 21 days in total.

MORNING TIME

As well as taking time to have that crucial time in prayer, we have also been taking the time to meditate on God's word in the morning. The morning can be used to spiritually set up the rest of our day in the best way. I like to take 10 minutes every morning to meditate on who I am in Christ and also review the personal words/goals the Lord has given to me.

NIGHT TIME/BEFORE BED

What we spend our time on before we go to sleep is critical. Our brains do not completely shut down when we sleep. It is thinking and sorting through what information we last gave it and what we have experienced throughout the day.

The thoughts we had will stay with us as we sleep and these very thoughts engrave the brain and the deeper the engraving, the stronger the thought. – Curry Blake

So each night take a few scriptures or affirmations and read them out loud and focus on the words. Read them strongly and passionately and take a few moments to think about how you can fulfill them the next day. The next morning take your time to wake up gently and document any dreams you had in a journal. Pay attention your first thoughts, write down how they make you feel.

BE A DOER OF THE WORD

Please note that it is not enough to just read the word and meditate on the word. We MUST be a doer of the word. I have read many books on cooking and baking (I love to produce great foods for my family) but real learning is only going to come via doing what I have read. Watching cooking shows on TV, will never match the learning experience of cooking it myself in my own kitchen. 1 Timothy 4:11-14 teaches us that we must give much attention to reading, exhortation, and doctrine so that our progress will be evident and seen by all to save ourselves and those around us.

BIBLE STUDY QUESTIONS

➢ Read through Joshua 1:8 what observations do you make from this verse.

➢ What are the benefits of meditating on the Words of God?

➢ Can you list the opposite effects of not meditating on God's word? What fruit do you see most in this mind renewal process?

➢ Read all the verses mentioned in the book of Psalms. What are the key times of day to meditate on God's word?

➢ Talk to the Lord today about how you can commit time in your day to practice meditating on the word more.

➢ We are to be doers of the word. Write three ways you can be more of a doer of the word.

SCRIPTURE PRAYER

Lord, I walk in faith today. Faith comes from hearing from You and doing what Your word requires me to do. As I renew my mind, I trust that transformation by faith is happening in me. Romans 10:17

AFFIRMATION

My heart is glad, and my glory [my inner being] rejoices, and my body too will dwell [confidently] in safety,

WEEK 6

CHRIST FOCUS 101

Day 37

CAPTIVE THOUGHTS VS VAIN IMAGINATIONS

Taking our thoughts captive, is in my opinion, the number 1 most potent method for renewing the mind.

2 Corinthians 10:4-6
4 For the weapons of our warfare are not [a]carnal but mighty in God for pulling down strongholds, 5 casting down arguments and every high thing that exalts itself against the knowledge of God, bringing every thought into captivity to the obedience of Christ, 6 and being ready to punish all disobedience when your obedience is fulfilled.

We have been given a spiritual weapon from God to pull down these thoughts that so frequently try to beset us. This spiritual weapon comes from the Lord and is empowered by Him and is not something we can do in our strength. This weapon enables us to take the thoughts and imaginations that do not line up with the word of God, thus taking down strongholds.

Pulling and casting down is the same Greek word which means to- lower down with violence or to demolish.

This is not something that should be taken lightly, as if we do not make proactively renewing our mind a habitual activity; we are liable to be inundated with toxic thoughts. But, there is hope!

We must at every opportunity capture the toxic thoughts and bring them into obedience. Sometimes for me, it has been a case of life or death, depression vs. freedom. I have been in so many situations where I have had no other choice but to fight. When I asked God why was I in such a place of warfare? You may remember from my testimony earlier that He told me it was not different trials I had faced, but it was the fact I have not taken the thoughts captive!

Our tool in this mighty fight is the scripture. The bible teaches that it is more powerful than a double-edged sword.

Hebrews 4:12-13

For the word of God is living and active. Sharper than any double-edged sword, it pierces even to dividing soul and spirit, joints and marrow. It judges the thoughts and intentions of the heart. Nothing in all creation is hidden from God's sight; everything is uncovered and exposed before the eyes of Him to whom we must give account.

The word of God is essential, as it is the only available tool that is able to divide between all the thoughts and intentions that we hold. It helps bring about truth as well as reveal false beliefs and toxic thoughts. When we take these thoughts captive we replace them with the word as many times as is necessary to achieve mind renewal.

So the key is that we have to take the time to be listening attentively to what we are thinking. I heard a phrase many years ago "to think about what you are thinking about" but it is necessary to understand what our thoughts are made of.

There are some notable areas that we should pay attention to, from whence toxic thoughts often come creeping in:

* Negative thoughts of the past/future - in the form of un-forgiveness, fear, guilt, and condemnation
* Memories of sin and disaster – past thoughts of sin should be there for testimony or forgiveness purposes, any other reasons in most cases are not thoughts that God wants us to meditate on.
* Vain imaginations – these are images that just tend to pop from the flesh or the enemy. They are not there because of a sin or a previous trauma but is a fiery dart.

Unfortunately when these toxic thoughts/memories arise we can tend to lean to our strength, over – sharing, over meditating on all that went wrong or walking into doubt, fear, unbelief, and shame, which becomes perpetual never-ending the cycle of living in the past.
If these thoughts are coming up, then this is when we know that we need to take them captive and exchange the lies for the truth that God is saying.

When these toxic thoughts come to the forefront (short – term memory) of our thinking they become more accessible to take captive, pull down and shift to the positive. Please note that I don't believe in going out searching for toxic thoughts or intentionally trying to re-live past trauma – the word is powerful enough as it is. If the Lord wants past memories to be brought forward to you, He will do it in His timing. The danger comes when we try to be intellectual/logical about these matters. Our true inner healing can only come from the power of the word and the Holy Spirit, and you have to believe the power of the word, you have to believe that God's Spirit is in you.

John 8:32
And you will know the truth, and the truth will set you free.

Psalm 147:3
He heals the brokenhearted and binds up their wounds.

BIBLE STUDY QUESTIONS

➢ How do you typically deal with negative thoughts, memories of sin/disaster and vain imaginations?

➢ Do you think dealing with these thoughts negatively or positively has been affecting your choices? If so. How?

➢ Through reading and observing John 8:32 and Psalm 147:3 What does God want to do for you?

➢ Hebrews 4 Tells us what the Word can do for us. Jot down the key benefits. Take the time to praise God for all the benefits you listed.

➢ Now take 5 minutes and close your eyes and take a few moments to imagine yourself experiencing these benefits.

SCRIPTURE PRAYER

Thank you, lord that any issues I have experienced have been through a lack of knowledge of understanding of how to pull down thoughts and taking them captive. I praise you that you have now given and are giving me a master class in renewing my mind today.

AFFIRMATION

My mind is being renewed. My thoughts are pure, and of good report; therefore I meditate on these pure things and of good report, things that bring joy to God and peace to my spirit.

WEEK 6

CHRIST FOCUS 101

Day 38

FIXED MINDSET VS GROWTH MINDSET

When I learned the concept of a fixed mindset and growth mindset, it helped me to be able to discern between what was of God and not of God. God has a growth mindset and wants us to have this same mindset. The flesh and the enemy want us to have a fixed mindset about life and to remain stuck.

Jeremiah 29:11
¹¹ For I know the thoughts that I think toward you, says the Lord, thoughts of peace and not of evil, to give you a future and a hope.

Proverbs 13:12a

Hope deferred makes the heart sick

Growth Mindset

A growth mindset stays focused on going forwards and upwards; it does not look at lack and believe that there is no way out. It seems that with God all things are possible. It does not mean that you do not see problems, but your view of them says that you see them as malleable and movable. This is where our mind is starting to line up with the mind of Christ when based on the word of God.

Fixed Mindset

A fixed mindset stays focused on what is not right; what is wrong with the situation and cannot move out from that perspective. This is a limited view and often comes when we are looking at our walk and in particular our personal goals, objectives, and agenda instead of God. This is where more of the toxic thoughts are going to sit.

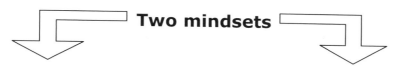

Two mindsets

Fixed	Growth
There is nothing I can do	I am going to grow
I will just take life as it comes	I can do all things through Christ
I am helpless	I am going to make it
It's too hard to continue	Greater is He that is in me
I accept reality as it is	Perfect love casts out fear, so I walk in love

I want to take a moment to address fear. A fixed mindset can lock us into a state of fear. It's a case of focusing on the fears of the unknown or making decisions from a 'lack perspective' and unbelief. I liken it to focusing on what we perceive as "God is not doing anything," rather than what God IS doing, or HAS already done.

How to make the shift?

We can see how we can be stuck in the pattern of negative thinking, so we are going to first have to re-position our mind to the reality of operating from what God has already given. Not trying to attain to get something from Him, but to recognize that we have already been given every spiritual blessing and everything we need to renew our minds.

We can do this through scripture journaling in written format when we take the time to observe the thoughts and tackle them. You may choose to work on a particular mountain for say 60 days.

But there also becomes a vital transition point where you can do this as you go about your day. When you are cultivating a rich relationship with the Lord, and when you are reading the word and praying often, you will naturally become more sensitive to thoughts that do not line up with the word of God. When you notice a toxic thought, you must take them captive.

Steps to taking thoughts captive
1. Start your day asking Holy Spirit to help you recognize and be sensitive to thoughts that do not line up with the word.

2. When you recognize a toxic thought speak positive scriptures and bring the thought into focus by praising God for the truth that the scriptures have shown you – Praise Him as you read and meditate.

3. Capture the positive thoughts also. The Bible says we should take our thoughts captive so take the positive ones as well and rejoice over these. Attach emotion/passion to the positive thoughts and affirmations that you use; this also increases connectivity between the brain and heart.

4. If there is a negative thought that is from any past wrongs, sins or disaster, then make sure you connect it to who you are in Christ today. You have the choice of what you do with that thought. Avoided toxic thoughts are going to do something whether you like it or not – either they are going to dictate your life, or you are going to have to take them captive and exchange them for truth.

5. Be very careful when speaking and repeating the toxic thoughts to others. How you discuss the thoughts can strengthen the thought and make it stronger. *Please note here that if you discern that you need help with thoughts that could cause you harm or harm to others, please do seek counsel from your Pastor or even contact myself and I can direct you further.

This process requires discipline, consistency and a level of boldness.

Boldness is required because you never know where you will be when a thought comes up that does not line up with who you are in Christ. You could be at the shopping mall, cooking supper or a dinner party. But you do have to take it captive as soon as possible – even if people look at you funny while you are talking to yourself *smiles*. We have to die to pride and reputation on this journey.

The more and more you repeat these activities the more the positive thoughts will take up mental capacity and the smaller the toxic thoughts will become.

We can speed up renewing the mind when we attach the thought to an emotion. So do so with fervency by bringing our emotions into it. Get fed up with the negative thoughts and attack them with force, pull them down, get active about it. When you meditate on the positive let yourself see the breakthrough happening to you, allow yourself to feel, the feelings of victory rising on the inside.

BIBLE STUDY QUESTIONS

➢ Read Colossians 3:2 what key observations can you make from this?

➢ Why should we not focus or meditate on earthly matters? What do you think are the characteristics of focusing on earthly matters? Look at James 3:15 as an example

➢ James 3:17 Gives a clear example of what we should be meditating on and how to discern heavenly wisdom. List the main areas.

➢ Why do you think it takes a dying to self to focus on heavenly/growth mindsets?

➢ What are three truths that you need to set your mind on today?

SCRIPTURE PRAYER

Father, because I have been crucified with Christ, my life is hidden in you! You can now call me Your chosen treasure, a chosen race, a royal priesthood, a holy nation, a person for Your possession. I can proclaim Your excellencies because You called me out of darkness into Your marvelous light.

AFFIRMATION

Thank you that through this journey You are teaching me how to take my thoughts captive properly. I sing out in an endless Hallelujah.

WEEK 6

CHRIST FOCUS 101

Day 39

TOTAL IMMERSION

Ephesians 4

[23] and be renewed in the spirit of your mind, [24] and that you put on the new man which was created according to God, in true righteousness and holiness.

Total Immersion is a process in which we submerge ourselves in the word. I believe that breakthrough comes from when we give ourselves entirely to the Lord. Immersing ourselves in the word, prayer, meditation and mind renewal and abiding has a direct result on the transformation we can experience. If we can get to a place of realizing that the negative strongholds of the mind we face are not God's plan for us and it is not even who we truly are, then we can walk in the position of an over-comer!

There are varying seasons of how much we need to immerse ourselves, and sometimes these are critical. But ignoring life issues is not going to change you. Trying to figure it out in your strength is not going to bring you peace. Whatever you ignore today will come back later and will have to be addressed one way or another.

Just like David, we want to establish a morning, afternoon and evening routine and to grow to the point of abiding and meditating throughout the day as we go about our daily lives. A habit of reading, studying, meditating, learning from Holy Spirit and putting in faith actions daily is the quickest way to renew our minds.

1 Timothy 4:15-16
[15] Meditate on these things; give yourself entirely to them, that your progress may be evident to all. [16] Take heed to yourself and to the doctrine. Continue in them, for in doing this you will save both yourself and those who hear you.

The Lord is calling us to immerse and give ourselves entirely.

It is not about how fast or quick we can renew our minds, but it is about how much we are immersing ourselves in truth. How much we are willing to stretch ourselves has a significant effect on our mind renewal. Even the smallest changes can make a huge difference in our lives. It is not easy and is a daily fight of faith but my friend, His grace is sufficient even when you feel weak and don't feel like you can continue. I have come to realize that the pressure we face when advancing forward in denying ourselves is proof that we are walking in the right direction.

Where my breakthrough came with mind renewal was when I stopped trying to fit mind renewal into my life and made my life about aligning myself to who I truly am in Christ.

The Lord has called us to lay down our lives and agenda to consecrate ourselves.

Knowing who you truly are in Christ can only be found by seeing yourself in the word of God continually and seeing who you are according to God's perspective.

James 1:22-25 ESV
But be doers of the word, and not hearers only, deceiving yourselves. For if anyone is a hearer of the word and not a doer, he is like a man who looks intently at his natural face in a mirror. For he looks at himself and goes away and at once forgets what he was like. But the one who looks into the perfect law, the law of liberty, and perseveres, being no hearer who forgets but a doer who acts, he will be blessed in his doing.

We need to be doers and not just hearers of the word; we have to keep our face centered on the word of God which is a mirror and a true reflection of who we are. Temptation, doubt, and not being consistent with the process, will cause us to turn away and forget who we are. This is falling into the enemy's trap, the same one that Adam and Eve fell into. So, total immersion means to keep focusing on the truth of the Word of God and who you are. Then as the last verse of James 1:22-25 says you will be blessed in all your doing.

Romans 12:1

I appeal to you; therefore, brothers, by the mercies of God, to present your bodies as a living sacrifice, holy and acceptable to God, which is your spiritual worship.

1 Peter 2:9 ESV

But you are a chosen race, a royal priesthood, a holy nation, a people for his own possession, that you may proclaim the excellencies of him who called you out of darkness into his marvelous light.

Colossians 3:3 ESV

For you have died, and your life is hidden with Christ in God.

We can talk a lot about taking off strongholds, but we have to put on the stronghold of Christ and the Kingdom of God.

HOW?

1 - Take the scripture and personalize it to you – imagine yourself in it or add your name into a place of connection to its context.

2 - Add emotion to how you speak the scripture. Emphasize each word of the scripture. As many times as there are words in the scripture just like the emphasizing scripture method I mentioned earlier, this will create stronger connections from 1 side of the brain to the other.

**Emotion, connected to the word and imagination
=
stronger emphasis and deeper roots of renewal.**

*Please do not forget the importance of visualizing yourself in the scripture.

SCRIPTURE PRAYER

Father, I immerse myself in your teaching and meditate on them always. Your word has become so real in my life that it bears fruit and everyone can see my progress. I give careful attention to my spiritual life and cherish every truth, for living by Your word releases an even more abundant life inside me. I am continually being renewed in the spirit of my mind; I put on my new self, created after Your likeness in true righteousness and holiness."
1 Timothy 4:15-16, Ephesians 4:23-24

AFFIRMATION

Thank you that through this journey You are teaching me how to take my thoughts captive properly. I sing out in an endless Hallelujah.

Bible Study Questions

➤ The Lord is calling us to immerse and give ourselves entirely to meditating on the word of God. Why do you think it is essential to immerse yourself in this way fully?

➤ What steps do you think you need to take to immerse yourself in the word of God?

➢ 1 Timothy 4:16 says to not only take heed to the word but also yourself. What do you think that means?

➢ James 1:22 teaches us that we need to be doers of the word and not just hearers. Take time to pray and ask the Lord how you can apply that to your life today? What does that look like for you?

WEEK 6

CHRIST FOCUS 101

Days 40-42

Take the time over the next few days to read through and pray these affirmations and scriptures from during the week. Don't forget to do the daily mind renewal plan.

SCRIPTURE PRAYERS

Lord, I walk in faith today. Faith comes from hearing from You and doing what Your word requires me to do. As I renew my mind, I trust that transformation by faith is happening on the inside of me.

Father, because I have been crucified with Christ, my life is hidden in you! You can now call me Your chosen treasure, a chosen race, a royal priesthood, a holy nation, a person for Your own possession. I can proclaim Your excellencies because You called me out of darkness into Your marvelous light.

Thank you, lord that any issues I have experienced have been through a lack of knowledge of understanding of how to pull down thoughts and taking them captive. I praise you that you have now given and are giving me a master class in renewing my mind today.

Father, I immerse myself in your teaching and meditate on them constantly. Your word has become so real in my life that it bears fruit and everyone can see my progress. I give careful attention to my spiritual life and cherish every truth, for living by Your Word releases an even more abundant life inside me. I am continually being renewed in the spirit of my mind; I put on my new self, created after Your likeness in true righteousness and holiness."

AFFIRMATIONS

My heart is glad, and my glory [my inner being] rejoices, and my body too will dwell [confidently] in safety,

My mind is being renewed. My thoughts are pure and of good report. I think on things that are pure and of good report, things that bring joy to God and peace to my spirit.

Thank you that through this journey You are teaching me how to take my thoughts captive properly. I sing out in an endless Hallelujah.

Thank you that through this journey You are teaching me how to take my thoughts captive properly. I sing out in an endless Hallelujah.

WEEK SEVEN

FIGHT THE GOOD FIGHT 101

Week Seven Daily Plan (Days 43-49)

Over the next two weeks, we want to start cementing what we have learned so far and ensured we have key practices and tools in place to ensure we finish well.

Quiet Time with the Lord
- Make sure you have your usual time with the Lord daily

Bible Study
- Read days 43-45 and complete the Bible study questions
- Days 46-49 Speak all the daily affirmations & scripture prayers

Renewing the Mind Daily Plan
- Continue the below mind renewal plan daily & 10 minutes review before you sleep.

Renewing the Mind Daily Suggestions

- Before you start, gather any materials or printables you are going to need

- Before you start mind renewal each day take a few moments in thanksgiving for what God is going to do in you as you renew your mind.

- At the end of each mind renewal session write down any revelations you received from the Lord in your personal journal or the mind renewal weekly tracker.

- Set the alarm for a minimum of 7 times a day ideally every hour and have armed with you scriptures that you are going to meditate on. You can also do your faith actions in these times.

- Before you go to bed take a scripture and meditate on this and see yourself in that scripture.

Renewing the Mind Daily Plan – Week Seven

*Day 43 Today pick a renewing of the mind tool that you sense is the best for you today

*Day 44 Let's use the Think On Model again today to focus on all you have achieved these past weeks

*Day 45 Complete a session of repeating and emphasizing 1 or 2 key scriptures based on the mountain you have been working on.

*Day 46 Look back over your journal entry on what your life will look back when you are transformed and spend time praising God and seeing yourself in that place

*Day 47- 49 Take all the truths in your journal & scripture prayers you received this week and meditate on these in your mind renewal time. You can also repeat any of the above tasks or from previous weeks on these days.

Faith Actions
- What action of faith is the Lord asking you to do today? This could be, declaring your scripture cards, mirror exercise or praying the scripture prayers.
- Do your faith action 7 times a day.

WEEK 7

FIGHT THE GOOD FIGHT 101

Day 43

Laboring into rest is the work it requires to trust God despite circumstances surrounding us. It requires a knowledge of everything we already have in Christ Jesus through the word and laboring to renew our minds to that truth. Then we receive a peace that surpasses all understanding. ~ Anon

RESTING IN CHRIST

Resting in Christ has been an area that has been truly dear to my heart. I have heard for many years others talking about resting in Christ and I perceived this as those fellow Christians who are just so calm and collected. While sure that this is often an outward manifestation, I had no idea how to enter into this place of resting in Christ exactly. I am by no means perfect, and revelation is progressive, but I have seen many breakthroughs and I believe that the ability to rest in God is directly connected with renewing the mind.

Laboring to enter into rest is what God is asking all of us to do.

The word discovers our condition

HEBREWS 4 is a fantastic chapter of the bible and explains it perfectly.

Hebrews 4:9-11

[9] There remains, therefore, a rest for the people of God. [10] For he who has entered His rest has himself also ceased from his works as God did from His.

[11] Let us, therefore, be diligent to enter that rest, lest anyone fall according to the same example of disobedience.

What is so amazing is that straight after verse 11 we enter into Paul describing the tools to enter into this rest which we have addressed previously in this book. The tools are the word of God as being a two edged sword. How amazing is our God!

One night I sat before the Lord in tears, I was tired of being tossed to and fro with dramas and cares in my life. Sure I knew that trials and tribulations were to come and to be expected even, but I did not like the way I would get into anxiety and stress and felt like I would be thrown back five steps. I spent a long time in prayer after a considerable number of life issues and just cried out to God for an answer.

I remember hearing the words "rest in me."

Believing in what God says and being obedient in what He has told us to do in life especially amid a storm, is the key to rest. The Lord wants you to be able to sit amidst storms and not be greatly moved. I desperately wanted this and have seen the fruit of practicing this, and I want the same for you too.

There are some amazing promises for abiding and resting in Christ. But you will notice that the scriptures state that we will have to 'labor' or some translations say 'make every effort" to enter into this rest. The Israelites were offered a similar kind of rest in the Promised Land, but they were not able to receive this message as the Bible says that it was not united with faith. But now we have Christ, a personal relationship with God as well as His word and Spirit, so we have everything available to enter in. I like to say that I have already entered this place of rest in the Spirit, but I now need to align my mind and body and soul into this realization.

Some truths I have discovered about entering into rest:

- Abiding in Christ and His word means that we are going to bear much fruit.
- Some areas of our lives are going to have to be cut, and some areas are going to require that we have to die to ourselves to bear much more fruit.
- It may be difficult at first, but it WILL bear the peaceful fruits of righteousness if we patiently endure.

- Remove stubbornness and hard-heartedness. Verse 7 teaches us that "Today if you hear His voice, do not harden your hearts."
- We have to trust God with everything in our lives, our appetites, our opinions, the opinions of others, our money, our marriages, etc. Entering into and experiencing rest comes from believing in the words He has spoken and written and being obedient to them.
- It is imperative that we do not look to lean on others or things before Christ for counterfeit rest, whether that be food, TV, drugs, people pleasing. Lack of entering that rest comes from somewhere that we didn't trust God which is evidenced by eventual disobedience.
- There is a special rest stored for you and me in Him. It is because of His love that He has made this available to us. So let us focus on love.
- His word is so powerful it will transform us if we just BELIEVE.

If I were to look back over times when I had been tossed about by the storms of life, I would see a common trend that I truly did not fully believe in faith what God said He would do for me. Like the Israelites, I saw the giants, and I doubted and got scared; then reacted by trying to take matters into my own hands via works. But when I have submitted to the Father, He has revealed to me in many ways what the real truth about all circumstances and what faith actions to take to connect with that truth. Most of these faith actions have not been easy – hence the laboring.

But without faith, it is impossible to [walk with God and] please Him, for whoever comes [near] to God must [necessarily] believe that God exists and that He rewards those who [earnestly and diligently] seek Him.
HEBREWS 11:6 AMP

The highest form of faith a man can enter into is rest. Rest is resisting from our performance, self-effort, and no more self-dependence.

Resting in God requires a level of trust, confidence, and reliance on something that is already finished and completed.

Without Him, we can do nothing. With Him, we can do all things.

While working towards resting, develop a focus on knowing that everything God has promised you will come to pass. Leaning and relying on what has already been done. Trusting in God and believing God's truth means that you have entered into rest.

The true reality is that because of the finished work of the cross we who do believe have entered into rest. Everything we face in life has been finished and dealt with at the foot of the cross. However, the way we react to a situation determines whether the trial is going to strengthen my resolve in Christ and be used as a tool for renewing my mind or, hold me at its mercy.

WE ARE RESTING BECAUSE IT IS FINISHED.

Jesus is our Sabbath rest and our source, and to Him, we depend on. We rest in what He has done. He has already given us the victory!

So why does it not always feel like that?

What we cannot see or feel works on our flesh to get us to question God's truth. Religion tricks us that if things are going to work out, we have to do the ten steps of works.

We have to renew our minds and lean on the grace of God when our flesh is weak.

What does laboring to enter into rest look like?

1. Let's say you are struggling with your finances, the bills are due, and they have to be paid. You are waiting on a paycheck and it's delayed.
2. You start to feel a bit worried. God tells you not to worry, and He will supply all your needs – you renew your mind on this, and you stand in truth.
3. When the bill collectors send you a reminder that states you have just two days to pay, you renew your mind again and believe that the money will come in time despite the pressure that is against you to believe differently.
4. You do a faith action to correspond with this stance of trust.
5. The laboring is where you continually renew your mind and refuse to agree with the negative. Then 10 minutes or a day later when the thought comes up again, you speak the same

truth and meditate on this truth. This is proactively renewing the mind.

6. The peace of God then comes to surpass all we can understand about that situation. We keep laboring to enter into that rest. Praise God and thank Him.

It is our job to pray, renew our minds and be in the word while taking faith actions that line up with the truth. Taking actions according to the word is a part of renewing the mind. You must keep standing in faith and believe as you renew your mind to the word and spend time using the tools mentioned, you would start to acknowledge and accept the truth more and more. Remember that the temptations you feel about giving up are the pressures being applied to your flesh to get you to do the opposite – self works. How we rest in this area will determine how we walk and live our daily lives.

BIBLE STUDY QUESTIONS

➤ Why did the Jew's struggle to enter into rest? Why did so many fall short of entering Canaan?

➤ Why do you think we need to labor? Why can it be such a struggle?

➤ Why is it critical to add faith actions to everything we believe?

➢ What is the number 1 tool to enter into rest and why is it so powerful?

➢ Look at your journey so far what do you need to resist so that you can enter into God's rest? What do you need to give up to enter into this rest?

SCRIPTURE PRAYER

Praise God that there are great rewards for resting in You and laboring into that rest. However, I thank you Lord that I can only do this with faith and believing that when You speak truth, it will come to pass in my life. I choose to seek you and your ways no matter the obstacle passionately and no matter what I see with my natural eyes that do not line up with your truth, I will trust.
Hebrews 11:6

AFFIRMATION

I relinquish all dispositions towards being moved, as my hope and provision is in Christ.

WEEK 7

FIGHT THE GOOD FIGHT 101

Day 44

REPETITION

Today we are going to focus on cultivating disciplines that will help to increase the effectiveness of our mind renewing process.

I used to hate the idea of repeating anything that went into too much depth. I just never saw the point – I love to hyper-focus on one point and just get it done – ONCE! *smiles.* But as I have grown to understand renewing the mind and study I have seen the absolute need for repetition. Our brains crave and need repetition to ensure a thought is fully cemented in us.

The more we meditate and repeat our brain creates more neural pathways and like branches on a tree they grow and grow and become stronger.

It takes revisiting a thought every 36 - 48 hours for it to become a memory. Hyper-focusing has its benefits, but when we need to get something into place, repetition is necessary daily. With church, we often receive a message on Sunday, and we won't revisit it, or maybe we will only do so just once in a small group. But I can guarantee that by the following Sunday most of us would've forgotten the main message. But by meditating on that word Monday, Tuesday, Wednesday and again Thursday this consistent pattern is going to enable us to retrain our minds.

In fact, by the 3rd day, a good way to test whether you have got a concept is to see whether you can share important truths to someone by day 3 of renewing your mind on a matter. This is why having a small group is so important to help you go over what you have learned in a larger setting. The early church used to meet daily – how fantastic!

The power of the 4th day!

It takes four days for the brain to slow down, turn around and change its mind on a negative matter. Full immersion over these four days is necessary as it can sometimes take years to stop going around the same mountains. This is not an easy task and many do struggle.

The more time you take to repeatedly meditate on a particular scripture the easier it is to bring it to the forefront of your memory when a matter comes up. The more times you do this over and over again, the more it forms a habit! Repetition is probably one of the most significant habits of success in renewing the mind.

Bible Study Questions

➢ Why is repetition in renewing the mind so important?

➢ Have you been committing to renewing the mind daily or several times a day? Do you see the results you need? List what you have been doing and is there anything you need to work on?

SCRIPTURE PRAYER

Father, how can I listen to Your word of Truth and not respond to it, for that would be the essence of self-deception. So I let Your word become like poetry written and fulfilled by my life! I listen to Your word and live out the message. I'm thankful I can look in the mirror and perceive how You see me in the mirror of Your word so that I never go out and forget my divine origin. I set my gaze deeply into the perfecting law of liberty and am fascinated by and respond to the truth I hear; I am strengthened by it—I experience God's blessing in all that I do!"
James 1:22-25

AFFIRMATION

You are my strength, strong Tower and the mighty fortress in me.

WEEK 7

FIGHT THE GOOD FIGHT 101

Day 45

FOCUS & CONCENTRATION

In renewing the mind, I have seen how there is a power in focus. I have to say here that I don't believe that it should take a decade to renew your mind in a particular area. However, growth, revelation, and practice are progressive and necessary. But my goal with this study is to show you that the word teaches us that the renewing of our minds can transform us and it doesn't have to take a lifetime!

The word transformed (which is the Greek word METAMORPHOMAI – to change from one form to another) is past tense, so that means there is an end point of when the transformation is complete.

There is a crucial purpose to renewing the mind that we should be able to test and prove the will of God in every area of our lives.

Focusing is the ability to zero in on one area of mind renewal with no distractions (as little as possible). Distractions can choke the word and the process of renewal. Focus can indeed speed up the process and remove the temptation to go back and forth on a matter. Peace is the essential quality that we need to remain focused — a type of peace of knowing that what we are doing is the most important matter.

The beauty of focus is that it increases revelation by the power of the Holy Spirit.

So I recommend when renewing the mind to FOCUS on one particular area or topic that the Lord has directed you to and limit as much as possible any distractions and the temptation to give your time to multiple areas. Assess the time wasters in your life and work to get them out while giving dedicated time to moving that mountain.

BIBLE STUDY QUESTIONS

➢ Metamorphami (transformed) is to change from one form to another just like the process of a Caterpillar to a Butterfly. What does the transformation in your area of struggle look like to you?

➢ What distractions have been trying to choke the word or truth from helping you remove this mountain?

➢ Mary and Martha show us the contrast in their preoccupation's Read Luke 10:38-42. Looking at their decisions, attitudes, and actions what do the verses reveal about their focus?

➢ What steps can you take to be more like Mary and less like Martha?

➢ What three steps can you take to be more dedicated and focused in this area?

➢ Why does focusing on God's word bring increased revelation?

➢ What are your top 3 time wasters? Ask Holy Spirit what He thinks when you spend time in these areas.

SCRIPTURE PRAYER

Father, I thank you for giving me complete rest, which allows me to cease from my works and follow Your example. Just as You celebrated Your finished work and rested in them. So then I must give my all and be eager to experience Your abundant rest filled life.

AFFIRMATION

No stumbling: I have great peace because I love God's law. Nothing causes me to stumble.

WEEK 7

FIGHT THE GOOD FIGHT 101

Days 46-49

Take the time over the next few days to read through and pray these affirmations and scriptures from during the week. Don't forget to do the daily mind renewal plan.

SCRIPTURE PRAYERS

Father, I thank you for giving me complete rest, which allows me to cease from my works and follow Your example. Just as You celebrated Your finished work and rested in them, so then I must give my all and be eager to experience Your abundant rest filled life.

Father, how can I listen to Your word of Truth and not respond to it, for that would be the essence of self-deception. So I let Your Word become like poetry written and fulfilled by my life! I listen to Your word and live out the message. I'm thankful I can look in the mirror and perceive how You see me in the mirror of Your word so that I never go out and forget my divine origin. I set my gaze deeply into the perfecting law of liberty and am fascinated by and respond to the truth I hear; I am strengthened by it—I experience God's blessing in all that I do!"

Praise God that there are great rewards for resting in You and laboring into that rest. However, I thank you Lord that I can only do this with faith and believing that when You speak truth, it will come to pass in my life. I choose to seek you and your ways no matter the obstacle with passion and no matter what I see with my natural eyes that does not line up with your truth, I will trust.

AFFIRMATIONS

You are my strength, strong Tower and the mighty fortress in me.

I relinquish all dispositions towards being moved, as my hope and provision is in Christ.

No stumbling: I have great peace because I love God's law. Nothing causes me to stumble.

WEEK EIGHT

TIME MANAGEMENT 101

Week Eight Daily Plan (Days 50-56)

Praise God for all the mighty work he has been doing in you. This week we talk about time management, setting goals and boundaries. Take some time this week in your spare time to download the goals worksheet on www.sophiatucker.com and think about future goals for renewing the mind and other areas of life going forward.

Quiet Time with the Lord
- Make sure you have your usual time with the Lord daily

Bible Study
- Read days 50-53 and complete the Bible study questions
- Days 54-56 Speak all the daily affirmations & scripture prayers

Renewing the Mind Daily Plan
- Continue the below mind renewal plan daily & 10 minutes review before you sleep.

Renewing the Mind Daily Suggestions

- Before you start, gather any materials or printables you are going to need

- Before you start mind renewal each day take a few moments in thanksgiving for what God is going to do in you as you renew your mind.

- At the end of each mind renewal session write down any revelations you received from the Lord in your personal journal or the mind renewal weekly tracker.

- Set the alarm for a minimum of 7 times a day ideally every hour and have armed with you scriptures that you are going to meditate on. You can also do your faith actions in these times.

- Before you go to bed take a scripture and meditate on this and see yourself in that scripture.

Renewing the Mind Daily Plan – Eight

*Day 51 Let's write out some more scripture prayers today based on 2-3 scriptures

*Day 52 Complete a session of repeating and emphasizing 1 or 2 critical scriptures based on the mountain you have been working on.

*Day 53 Talk to Holy Spirit today about what He thinks, see's and feels about your journey thus far.

*Day 54- 56 Take all the truths in your journal & scripture prayers you received this week and meditate on these in your mind renewal time. You can also repeat any of the above tasks or from previous weeks on these days.

Faith Actions
- What action of faith is the Lord asking you to do today? This could be, declaring your scripture cards, mirror exercise or praying the scripture prayers.
- Do your faith action 7 times a day.

WEEK 8
TIME MANAGEMENT 101

Day 50

MANAGING YOUR TIME

Renewing the mind is a labor intensive process. It simply is not just reading the word or attending a church service.

On the one hand, our flesh wants things to take as little time as possible; on the other side, renewing the mind is very simple in principle but requires an investment of time. We live in a fast-paced world that wants everything as a quick fix with immediate results. But renewing the mind is different.

I am a firm believer that the amount of time and intensity you dedicate to renewing the mind determines the degree of which you can see the radical transformation.

The word is clear; we will be transformed when we renew our minds. Many fail, or are not consistent when it comes to renewing the mind either because they do not fully understand what true mind renewal is or what is involved in the process and are not willing to put in the time for this process.

Life changes just like with the seasons, weather, day or night. For many of us our children go back to school, we have vacations, busier times at work, new promotions or just a family crisis that requires more of our time. It is effortless to keep on renewing the mind when it fits into our secure and simple schedules but what happens when things get tougher, busier? Well, there is a dual revealing in these seasons it often reveals more areas that we need to renew our mind about, but also how often we struggle to adapt to these life changes. But this is precisely when it is time to renew our minds with greater vigor.

Firstly we have to look at our goals and objectives in life. Why are we undertaking this process and why is it necessary? Write down the vision and make it clear.

➤ Write down your motivation for continuing in this journey of mind renewal.

SCRIPTURE PRAYER

Holy Spirit, remind me to be very careful of how I live, not being like those with no understanding, but I choose to live honorably with true wisdom, for I am living in evil times. I take full advantage of every day as I spend my life for Your purpose. And because I don't live foolishly, I have the discernment to understand Your will fully."
Ephesians 5:15-17

AFFIRMATION

I decide to live honourably in my use of time, I use my time wisely

WEEK 8
TIME MANAGEMENT 101

Day 51

TIME WASTERS

Removing time wasters out of my life has over the years been a struggle for me. Time wasters are things like TV, YouTube, social media, long telephone conversations. Often we will say that we just don't have the time to renew our minds, but we do have time to spend time on the above. However, whether we know it or not, our mind is being fed all kinds of information and can sometimes make the work we are trying to accomplish more difficult.

In particular, when I used to watch soap operas and would get emotionally involved in the fictional lives of made up characters, it became bondage and not to mention a form of busybodying of other people's lives. It is not my job here to tell you what you should or should not remove or limit out of your life. However, I do encourage you to analyze and manage your time and your life in a way that pleases God.

Ephesians 5:15-17

Look carefully then how you walk, not as unwise but as wise, making the best use of the time because the days are evil. Therefore do not be foolish, but understand what the will of the Lord is.

Be encouraged that no matter the season you are in, you can still renew your mind, in fact, I STRONGLY encourage, that the busier and more difficult the season, then more time should be given to getting our thinking in line with our Father's.

BIBLE STUDY QUESTIONS

➢ How much time do you typically give to renewing the mind at the moment when addressing the mountain you are facing? Do you think you are starting to see a transformation?

➢ Are you struggling with consistency? If so what can you put in place now to establish more routine? Can you adapt your schedule?

➢ List your top 3 time wasters. Do you think these are permissible and beneficial or non-beneficial? Are they aiding your spiritual growth or causing hindrances?

➤ List 3 real ways you can eliminate time-wasting today and over the next remaining weeks.

➤ Ephesians 5:15-17 warns us that the days are evil and to not be foolish. What do you think is the will of God for you in this season?

ASSIGNMENT

Look at the schedule in the appendix (or download from the website www.sophiatucker.com) and take a day to jot down what you do in all those hours. In the following section, we will analyze and see if we can better manage our time and add in some solid times of mind renewing.

SCRIPTURE PRAYER

Thank you, Father that I can walk with great care and purpose, not as a fool would walk carelessly in life. I can redeem the time in these last days. Thank you for giving me your wisdom, so that I can understand what your will is concerning the management of my time.

AFFIRMATION

I number my days and apply my heart to God's wisdom.

WEEK 8
TIME MANAGEMENT 101

Day 52-53

SETTING GOALS & BOUNDARIES

Do you have goals? Do you know where you are going in the next three months, five years or 10 years? Goals enable you to put your faith into a specific place in time and help you to form a picture of what it could look like when you get there. What has God asked you to accomplish in your life? When we get a clear insight into this, we can start to honestly ask God what is hindering His plans for your life.

Fear was one of those areas that got in the way of what God wanted to do in my life. I had to take at least a solid year renewing my mind on many areas of fear. Knowing that God had called my husband and me to public ministry meant that I had to conquer these lies of people pleasing and fears of the unknown.

Whether or not you know what God has in store for you right now, one thing is for sure that when we renew our minds to the word of God we start to know the will of God for our lives. Then we have to steward the call that God has placed on us.

Setting goals for renewing the mind

As renewing the mind can be time intensive I have found great success in setting goals for renewing the mind. Through prayer and spending time enquiring of the Lord, you can find out your mountains and how often He wants you to dedicate to this area of renewal.

The importance of setting goals is to develop a strategy to move your mountain with the tactics and tools of the Spirit and to establish a deadline for its total removal from your life. As I have said previously it is not God's will to see you struggle in bondage to a particular mountain in your life.

When establishing goals, it is of utmost importance that this is done with the Lord in much prayer and maybe an accountability partner.

GOALS MUST BE S.M.A.R.T!

S – Specific, Significant and stretching

- Identify the specific area you need to renew your mind on for example the mountain of fear could include (man-pleasing, social anxiety, submitting to authority, fear of failure or the unknown).
- What significant impact will these make in your life once transformation starts to manifest? What impact are these mountains having on your life now?

M- Measurable, Meaningful and Motivational

- Identify how many areas under that mountain need tackling.
- Gather the scriptures that encourage you and will arm you on this journey
- What will life look like once you have achieved transformation?

A – Achievable, Agreed upon with God, Faith action – orientated

- Did I forget to mention prayer again? *smiles* I just want to remind you again that goals in this area must line up with the word of God and in much prayer.
- What practical actions do you need to take? Re-evaluate your schedule? Carve some daily time out for yourself and God? Set up reminders. What Faith actions can you take that will see you walking out the truths you are renewing your mind with?

R – Realistic, Reasonable

- Think about the time it is going to take to commit to renewing your mind to your mountain. How much time does God require you to spend on this?
- Whatever decision you make, you and God know how essential it is to move your mountain totally. For some of us, we are at crisis point and need to give over lots of time, for others, 15 minutes a day is more than suitable. I do think it is a personal – spirit-led decision.

T – Time-based, Time-bound, Trackable

- How often are you going to renew your mind? How long are you going to give each time? When I took a year to demolish fear in my life, this was something God spoke to me about personally. It is something I had struggled with for 36 years. I still have a few areas to work on, but praise God I am so much further than I ever thought possible. After that year I was also more open and sensitive for the Lord to show me areas I had not seen before.

- Tracking your mind renewal journey is very useful! Are you going to journal your progress (recommended)? Having an accountability partner is also a fantastic idea. Asking them to check on you periodically is a great motivator. Write down each of the renewing the mind tools you are going to use.

Many people fail in life, not from lack of ability, or brains, or even courage, but simply because they have never organized their energies around a goal. Eibert Hubbard

BIBLE STUDY QUESTIONS

You have had considerable time during this study to learn and practice implementing our mind renewal tools. This study has been guiding you through the past eight weeks but what do you do when this study is finished? Let's start planning for the future.

- ➤ Are you planning to take on a new mountain to renew your mind about after this study? If so what will it be? Or do you feel like you need to work on this current mountain a bit longer?

➢ Take some time to start setting some smart goals for the remainder of this study and after that. Look at the goal setting worksheet in the appendix or download from my website.

➢ Also look at your actual schedule and highlight areas that are time wasters or could be better replaced with times of mind renewal. Create a new schedule based on your unique goals and identified time wasters.

SCRIPTURE PRAYER

Father God, thank you that I can write down the visions that I have received from you for my life. I appreciate that with your help, I have the power to run towards my goals. I wait on you Lord, and you renew my strength again today.

AFFIRMATION

I may not know the exact specifics over the future, but I stand in confidence in You my God and who You are. I shall not miss the 'in the meantime seasons' as they build greatly in our lives, marriage, and children. Your timing is perfect. I don't mind waiting.

WEEK 8
TIME MANAGEMENT 101

Days 54 – 56

Take the time over the next few days to read through and pray these affirmations and scriptures from during the week. Don't forget to do the daily mind renewal plan.

SCRIPTURE PRAYER

Holy Spirit, remind me to be very careful of how I live, not being like those with no understanding, but I choose to live honorably with true wisdom, for I am living in evil times. I take full advantage of every day as I spend my life for Your purpose. And because I don't live foolishly, I have the discernment to understand Your will fully."
Ephesians 5:15-17

Thank you, Father that I can walk with great care and purpose, not as a fool would walk carelessly in life. I can redeem the time in these last days. Thank you for giving me your wisdom, so that I can understand what your will is concerning the management of my time.

Father God, thank you that I can write down the visions that I have received from you for my life. I appreciate that with your help, I have the power to run towards my goals. I wait on you Lord, and you renew my strength again today.

AFFIRMATION

I decide to live honourably in my use of time, I use my time wisely

I number my days and apply my heart to God's wisdom.

I may not know the exact specifics over the future, but I stand in confidence in You my God and who You are. I shall not miss the 'in the meantime seasons' as they build greatly in our lives, marriage, and children. Your timing is perfect. I don't mind waiting.

WEEK NINE

STANDING STRONG 101

Week Nine Daily Plan (Days 57-63)

Friend you have now reached the final week of this study! CONGRATULATIONS! Now, this week I want you to take the reins more and take the time to choose the methods of mind renewal you want to do each day. Please write in your journal this week all the changes that have happened over these last nine weeks.

If you feel like the mountain is still holding on a little take more time to ensure you renew your mind by focusing on truths you have discovered over the last nine weeks. Again praise the Lord for this journey.

Quiet Time with the Lord
- Make sure you have your usual time with the Lord daily

Bible Study
- Read days 57-59 and complete the Bible study questions
- Days 60-63 Speak all the daily affirmations & scripture prayers

Renewing the Mind Daily Plan
- Continue the below mind renewal plan daily & 10 minutes review before you sleep.

Renewing the Mind Daily Suggestions

- Before you start, gather any materials or printables you are going to need

- Before you start mind renewal each day take a few moments in thanksgiving for what God is going to do in you as you renew your mind.

- At the end of each mind renewal session write down any revelations you received from the Lord in your personal journal or the mind renewal weekly tracker.

- Set the alarm for a minimum of 7 times a day ideally every hour and have armed with you scriptures that you are going to meditate on. You can also do your faith actions in these times.

- Before you go to bed take a scripture and meditate on this and see yourself in that scripture.

Renewing the Mind Daily Plan – Nine

*Day 57 – 63 Take the time to practice using the most beneficial tools for mind renewal for you each day.

*Ask the Lord what He wants you to implement after this study.

Faith Actions

- What action of faith is the Lord asking you to do today? This could be declaring your scripture cards, mirror exercise or praying the scripture prayer. Whatever you choose make sure it is just 1 minute long and write it down in your journal or the accountability worksheet and move to step 5

WEEK 9

STANDING STRONG

Day 57

SET A GUARD OVER YOUR SENSES
(Protecting what we watch, see, hear)

Our senses are so powerful, and they open a gateway to our heart, soul, and minds therefore how we look after them can have a positive or negative impact on our journey of mind renewal.

This is an area that I had struggled with for years as I just really and truly felt that this was an area that was too difficult to tackle. I have by no means reached a state of perfection in my mind, but I have achieved a place of surrender, where I am willing to give all things over to the Lord.

Scientifically our senses gather all information to be stored in the electromagnetic functions of our brain. These then dictate our daily actions. I want to focus on what we are hearing and what we are watching or seeing.

Let's look at some scriptures on this. Grab a Bible and let's go through the word together.

Watching

Matthew 6:22-23 or Luke 11:33-36 AMP

Here the Lord is showing us that we need to keep our eyes clear or spiritually perceptive, as what we let through our eyes has a direct impact on our body for good or bad.

Psalm 101:3, Job 31:1a AMP

David and Job made a covenant that they would not set anything worthless or wicked before their eyes.

Matthew 5:29 AMP

Here the Lord is saying that we must remove from our lives anything that can be a source of temptation in particular via our eyes.

Psalm 119:37 AMP

Again David says that he will turn his eyes away from worldly, meaningless things that would distract him and I believe asking the Lord to let His heavenly priorities become his own. Therefore, restoration and renewal were possible.

Hearing

Romans 10:17

Our faith/ what we believe comes from what we are hearing. Ideally, our hearing should come from the word of Christ, generating faith.

Luke 8:18/Mark 4:24

Let us be careful HOW we hear and also let us pay close attention to what we are listening.

James 1:19-27

Such a true scripture, to be quick to hear and to put away wickedness, while also receiving with meekness the engrafted word of God. To be engrafted means to be built into, so to continue into the lasting success we must develop the mind of Christ into our thinking using His word.

John 10:27

We are God's children, and we can hear His voice to follow Him.

When I was struggling with conquering the spirit of fear and anxiety over my life, the Lord showed me that part of the renewing process that was being affected was based on what or who I was listening to and watching. I would spend a lot of time watching disaster movies and fear-driven/suspense type shows, this was apparently not helping me and was creating toxic images and thoughts that were not helping my journey to renewal.

I want also to note that the opinions of friends and family - while intended to support us - can also go precisely against what we believe. Have you ever been trying to stay focused on eating in the right way according to boundary lines you have set? Only to have well-meaning family members state "oh go on it doesn't matter, eat the cake; it's just one bite." And after enough time of listening to that over and over again, your thoughts start to align up with the other person's opinion instead of what God has said.

Jesus had a similar experience when Peter spoke something that was opposite to the purposes of God. The Lord still loved Peter completely but corrected him promptly, as Peter did not know from what mind he was speaking. As his words were not God's will but were focused on people pleasing. Mark 8:31-34

Then Jesus said one of the most powerful statements:

Mark 8:34 - 37

34 When He had called the people to Himself, with His disciples also, He said to them, "Whoever desires to come after Me, let him deny himself, and take up his cross, and follow Me. 35 For whoever desires to save his life will lose it, but whoever loses his life for My sake and the gospel's will save it. 36 For what will it profit a man if he gains the whole world, and loses his own soul? 37 Or what will a man give in exchange for his soul?

We MUST take up our cross with a willingness to endure whatever may come and what that may look like.

This is a time where we have to stand with the full armor of God and labor to enter into true rest, despite the challenges which we may face. We can use those challenges as an opportunity to draw even closer on God's truth.

I have seen time and time again that those who have an awesome breakthrough in renewing the mind are those who decide to remove time wasters temporarily or even permanently out of their lives, things that so easily beset them to sin or distract them from focusing on the truth.

We may have to practice saying 'No thank you' more often to people. We may have to start saying if I am trying to renew my mind and to stay pure and away from sexual immorality, I am going to have to put a stop to watching romantic films or reading those romance novels. Is it easy? No. Is it worth it? Absolutely.

It requires all three main parts of our being to renew the mind. The spirit, God's word, the soul (Our thoughts) and the Body (the actions we take).

SO WHAT DOES THAT LOOK LIKE?

For instance, if I am trying to deal with overcoming gossip:

1. I am going to find the scriptures relevant to that area, i.e. Psalm 141:3 Set a guard, O LORD, over my mouth; Keep watch over the door of my lips.
2. I am going to write down the scripture and do some scripture journaling in the same area.
3. Next, I am going to spend some time meditating on this scripture and look at how God wants me to handle gossip.
4. Indirect faith action – I am going to stop reading the gossip magazines, watching the gossip chat shows.
5. Direct faith action – Before I speak to say a particular friend, I am going to spend a few more minutes meditating on this area, then I am going to meet with the friend, and I am going to be quick to listen and slow to speak.

By connecting the word of God to your; thoughts, words, and faith actions you will be linking together as many parts of your being as possible. This is probably one of the most understated powerful secrets to renewing our minds. In doing this we engage our whole being in this process, loving the Lord with our whole heart, mind, soul, and strength. The more we utilize a holistic approach to renewing the mind the more powerful the results will be, no matter what the mountain is.

The goal is that when the pressures of life come upon you, you will only be squeezed closer into Him and what will come out of you in the pressure, will be His word, mixed with faith.

The day I realized that my actions could proactively renew my mind was an absolute game-changer!

BIBLE STUDY QUESTIONS

➤ Why is it so important to protect our eye gates and ear gates? (Matthew 6:22, Psalm 101:3, Proverbs 20:12, Luke 8:15-18)

➤ Why must we place a guard over our lips? *Proverbs 18:2, Psalm 141:3, Matthew 12:35-37)*

➤ List 6 ways you believe you can protect what you see and hear?

➤ A covenant is a promise and agreement we make with God. Take some time in prayer and ask God where He may want you to make a covenant with Him regarding your eye and ear gates and for how long?

SCRIPTURE PRAYER

Lord I make a choice today to remove distractions from my life that dishonour You. But not just dishonour as all things are permissible but not beneficial therefore help me to see those things in my life that do not benefit the plans You have for me. I refuse to serve two masters I choose to serve the One and only true God and that is You Yahweh.

Matthew 6:23-24

AFFIRMATION

I am putting to death and depriving my flesh of its desires. And anything that gets in the way of my full devotions to God.

WEEK 9

STANDING STRONG

Day 58

GIVING TO OTHERS, SERVING OTHERS INTERCESSION TEACHING & ACCOUNTABILITY

When I first became a christian, I went straight into being part of a worship team. Some of the elders struggled with the idea that new Christians should not be in the worship team. However, I had an experience of worshiping the King and learning the Word of God and His nature through worship. I also was being led by my spiritual mother who was also the worship leader.

Over the years I began to honestly believe that if I was not serving in this capacity, I am not sure if I would've kept my faith. I came to Christ with a lot of strongholds, and they needed to be removed from my life. Through leading others in worship, I learned to lay down my agenda and my life. Was I perfect? In the natural NO! Did I make many mistakes? Absolutely. As the years have gone on, I've come to realize that serving and giving to others in the area you need renewal in is one of the powerhouses of faith actions and using them to renew our mind and change our perspective.

The same for me came when I began to lead Bible studies and now a wonderful group of ladies seeking to renew their minds and transform their lives for the glory of God. Teaching has cemented my beliefs deeper and even by writing this book it has given me further revelation.

I strongly encourage you to do some type of serving where you can apply the teaching you have learned that as you give, aids your renewing journey.

Luke 6:38

Giving to others will enable God to pour back everything you gave and more back into your lap.

Mark 10:45

For even Jesus came not to be served but to serve others

It may be through being someone's accountability partner. You may be at a higher level of living in a renewing mindset, which empowers you to teach biblical principles to someone else. There are different levels to this.

When you are just seeing the beginning of the power of utilizing God's word to transform your life you can begin to share your testimony and what God is doing in you. Then it gets to a point where we are so convinced, so passionate; you are living out the evidence of transformation so that when you teach or serve others in this area, you are fully confident. Even just encouraging another person and carrying each other's burdens the scriptures say we will fulfill the law of Christ. Galatians 6:2

But this, of course, is not just limited to the topic of mind renewal it is whatever you have been focusing on - weight loss, the power of fasting, marriage, overcoming anger or Gods view on finances.

Proverbs 22:9a

He who is generous/bountiful will be blessed.

When you are looking for who you can bless, then you will also be blessed. You don't have to wait until you are fully renewed in an area. That is the point; it reinforces the word of God in your life when you share it with others in Love. Do you remember when you first got saved? If you were anything like me, I went around telling everybody about Jesus and the Kingdom. It was reinforcing my beliefs and my faith. When I came up with areas, I did not know the answer to I went back in the word and researched further. I still do this now. My prayer is that you will practice walking this out in your daily life. This could be part of your faith actions.

Intercession & Prayer for Others

Intercession is the best gift we can give another person. It is one of the core ways we can serve loved ones and friends in our lives. Luke 22:32 Jesus prayed for Peter's faith that it would not fail. Then what I love in this scripture is that when Peter was strengthened, he was to support His brothers in the faith. Spending time to stand in prayer for others is beautiful and powerful for you both.

Matthew 18:19-20

19 "Again[a] I say to you that if two of you agree on earth concerning anything that they ask, it will be done for them by My Father in heaven. 20 For where two or three are gathered together in My name, I am there in the midst of them."

Ephesians 4:25

25 Therefore, putting away lying, "Let each one of you speak truth with his neighbor," for we are members of one another.

BIBLE STUDY QUESTIONS

➤ Read Luke 6:38. Often this verse is relating to giving tithes and offerings. But for the purposes of renewing the mind, when sharing with or encouraging others how can this make an impact on your journey?

➤ What will be the benefit to your fellow brother and sister in Christ?

➢ Read Romans 12:7-8 which speak of encouraging others with your spiritual gifts. Who can you reach out to this week to support? How can you best go about doing this?

➢ Do you have a support group or accountability partner? If so, how can you strengthen your relationship with your partners/team?

➢ Ask the people surrounding you what changes they have seen in you over the last several weeks?

SCRIPTURE PRAYER

Lord, lead me to stay committed to accountability in this journey I know that love empowers me to carry the burdens of my brother or sister. As we cover one another in prayer and counsel strengthen us to stay the course. As we pray together in your name I am grateful to You because You are right here with us now, even in our midst. In Jesus' Name, amen.

Matthew 18:19-20

AFFIRMATION

I will serve my family, friends and others unselfishly today in joy and strength and energy from resting in love with You. I can do all things through Christ who strengthens me.

WEEK 9

STANDING STRONG

Day 59

CRISIS POINT

Intensive Renewing the Mind (4-day intensive program)

I believe firmly that when going through specific trials, it is imperative to dedicate extensive and intensive time of fellowship with the Lord through renewing of the mind. It can range from the death of a loved one, a financial crisis, and health crisis or just you have found yourself in a place you don't want to be in your walk with God. There is a time to dig deep and draw all our strength from the Lord when we do not feel like we have any left. When we experience weakness, He is strong.

As I explained at the beginning of the book my testimony of breaking free from panic attacks came from an intensive time with the Lord. It had reached boiling point for me, and I was in a situation where if it had not been for the Lord I don't know what would have happened. The Lord showed me at that time that He would use me to help set others free. Now, this program won't necessarily completely eradicate all the issues you are facing, but it can defiantly give you the kick start and boost you need. Submit to the Lord completely!

So I want to recommend a plan for a Full immersion intensive plan. Now all of this is dependent on the time that you have available and how much you desperately need breakthrough. You may be working full time, or a mum with lots of little ones, or a husband with crazy work commitments. Obviously, I would say wherever possible carve out time for this process whether it requires a weekend or a few days, only you would know by the leading of the Spirit.

A 4 DAY INTENSIVE PLAN

DISCLAIMER

You must not rely on the information in this book as an alternative to medical advice from your doctor or other professional healthcare providers. If you have any specific questions about any medical matter, you should consult your doctor or another professional healthcare provider. If you think you may be suffering from any medical condition, you should seek immediate medical attention. You should never delay seeking medical advice, disregard medical advice or discontinue medical treatment because of information in this book.

Top Tips

- Pick an area or lie that you need to focus on. Scientifically it takes four days of full focus on an area to start turning your thoughts around. This is just a kick start process. You will need to maintain and work on this after 3 or 4 days.

- You have 24 hours in a day with let's say 7 hours sleep, with 5 hours dedicated to cooking, dressing eating. That's 12 hours left a day now depending on whether you work or not that takes a substantial amount of time. But if you are focusing on doing this on a weekend or holiday, then you can dedicate more significant time to this process.

- To the young mothers get some help to look after the little ones. If you can't, then set the children up with some activities that they can do independently.

- Prep your meals or batch cook in advance or even better still take some time to fast.

- You need to clear out all distractions. All things are permissible but not beneficial. So as mentioned prior over the time you have committed to the Lord for this process you need to identify time wasters. TV, social media, Facebook, idle chat, etc.

- Get plenty of sleep unless the Lord asks you to enter into all night prayer (This is something we do in our home once a week). The Lord loves to speak to us in our dreams. Our brains are still active but our bodies have shut down, and we can hear so much more clearly.

- Let your accountability partner, mentor or spiritual leader know your plans. I offer 1 to 1 coaching through this process and many other areas. If you need support, feel free to email me on info@sophiatucker.com
- Have a space in your home that you can have minimal disturbance and can have quiet time. If you cannot do so all day, that's okay, try at least to get several times throughout the day to be by yourself with God.
- Have worship or a prayer room like IHOP-KC playing throughout the house during the day.
- Scriptures played to music or what some would call soaking music is also very powerful.
- All the activities I will explain below are a suggestion only. This is what worked for me and others. But please take the time to ask the Lord what is best for you in your particular situation.

SUGGESTED DAILY PRACTICE

IN THE MORNING

1. Wake up slowly with no loud alarms try to focus on your first thoughts as you wake up and journal these.
2. Before your feet touch the floor take some time to worship God or speak to the Lord.
3. Prayer time with the Lord.
4. Spend time affirming and speaking who you are in Christ. Start declaring truths about the day before you.
5. Meditate on the attributes of God and His nature.
6. Make sure you take time to listen before the Lord and Journal everything.
7. Do you have a prayer or intercession list for others? Take the time to go through this with the Holy Spirit.
8. Talk to yourself every day the truths and word of God.

DURING THE DAY

1. Set the alarm for a minimum of 7 times a day ideally every hour and have armed with you scriptures that you are going to meditate on.
2. The other times of the day you need to look back over your journal notes of scriptures or revelations you have received and speak to the Lord about them.
2 Have a substantial time in the middle of the day to pray also.
3 If you are fasting, every time you would normally eat take time to be in the word.
4 Every time a thought comes up that is opposite to the truth you need to use one or several of the tools mentioned in this book to renew the mind.
5 When you see difficulties come up in the day write them down and state the date and time and write next to it the testimony of God goodness and breakthrough after each one as they appear.

EVENING

1. Take time to be silent before the Lord.
2. Journal your day and retake a look over everything you have written.
3. Write a list of thanksgiving for the day.
4. Take a key scripture and meditate on this and see yourself in that scripture.
5. Sleep with worship in the background or scripture lullabies. You can find these on YouTube.
6. As soon as you wake up the next morning, wake slowly and journal what you have received.

SCRIPTURE PRAYER

With your help Father, I refuse to let anger cause sin in my life, I refuse to let falsehood develop in me, Father; let your truth develop in me mightily. I praise you God that you have given me the power by your Spirit and Word to give no opportunity to the devil, the enemy has no victory, Jesus has the victory and I share in His victory because of the cross, and the resurrection.

Thank you Jesus for sealing me with your precious Holy Spirit. Amen.

Ephesians 4:21-30

AFFIRMATION

Your Word is my medicine because it is Spirt and it is life to me.

WEEK 9

STANDING STRONG

Day 60-63

Take the time over the next few days to read through and pray these affirmations and scriptures from during the week. Don't forget to do the daily mind renewal plan.

SCRIPTURE PRAYERS

Lord I make a choice today to remove distractions from my life that dishonour You. But not just dishonour as all things are permissible but not beneficial therefore help me to see those things in my life that do not benefit the plans You have for me. I refuse to serve two masters I choose to serve the One and only true God and that is You Yahweh.

Matthew 6:23-24

Lord, lead me to stay committed to accountability in this journey I know that love empowers me to carry the burdens of my brother or sister. As we cover one another in prayer and counsel strengthen us to stay the course. As we pray together in your name I am grateful to You because You are right here with us now, even in our midst. In Jesus' Name amen.

Matthew 18:19-20

With your help Father, I refuse to let anger cause sin in my life, I refuse to let falsehood develop in me, Father; let your truth develop in me mightily. I praise you God that you have given me the power by your Spirit and Word to give no opportunity to the devil, the enemy has no victory, Jesus has the victory and I share in His victory because of the cross, and the resurrection.

Thank you Jesus for sealing me with your precious Holy Spirit. Amen.

Ephesians 4:21-30

AFFIRMATIONS

I am putting to death and depriving my flesh of its desires. And anything that gets in the way of my full devotions to God.

I will serve my family, friends and others unselfishly today in joy and strength and energy from resting in love with You. I can do all things through Christ who strengthens me.

Your Word is my medicine because it is Spirt and it is life to me.

Conclusion

Congratulations on completing this 9-week program and bible study!

My heart and prayers for you during this journey was that no matter what you have been facing in life that you have had the opportunity to experience the power of mind renewal. One of the truths that I have learned during my journey is that revelation is progressive meaning that God is going to continue to speak to you about the mountain that I pray has been destroyed (or at least moved).

Renewing our minds to the mind of Christ in all areas of our lives takes time, and we want to stay focused and committed to laying down everything before God and taking every thought captive.

As you reflect this week take the time to ask the Lord what area He would want you to focus on next. I pray that you will have at least found some tools that you can now have in your arsenal as you battle. Not only this but that you are confident in why and how you should renew your mind. It is not a choice; it is a necessity for life.

It has been an honor and privilege to share with you this book. I would love to hear from you and how this study has impacted your life or if you have any further questions. Please contact me via email on info@sophiatucker.com.

Thank you, Father, for my dear brother and sister in Christ, who has been on this journey with me seeking victory and breakthrough in their lives. May they be transformed for your glory and may they be able to live a life fully laid down and in love-based obedience to You. This I pray in the mighty name of Jesus Christ. Amen

All my love

Sophia

APPENDIX

Week One Daily Plan (Days 1-7)

Week one begins with us renewing our minds on renewing our minds. It sounds funny, but if we don't take this first vital step the remainder of the journey will be difficult. You need to know why you are renewing the mind and the power there is through the Word of God as you are going to want to hold on to these truths. I know you probably really want to address your area of renewal and that will come in week 3, but take these first critical steps this week and next week, and we will genuinely be laying down some great foundations.

Each day

Quiet Time with the Lord

- Make sure you have your usual time with the Lord daily

Bible Study

- Read days 1 - 4 and complete the Bible study questions
- Days 5 - 7 speak all the daily affirmations & scripture prayers

Renewing the Mind Daily Suggestions

- Before you start, gather any materials or printables you are going to need

- Before you start mind renewal each day take a few moments in thanksgiving for what God is going to do in you as you renew your mind.

- At the end of each mind renewal session write down any revelations you received from the Lord in your personal journal or the mind renewal weekly tracker.

- Set the alarm for a minimum of 7 times a day ideally every hour and have armed with you scriptures that you are going to meditate on. You can also do your faith actions in these times.

- Before you go to bed take a scripture and meditate on this and see yourself in that scripture.

Renewing the Mind Daily Plan – Week One

- This week we will be focusing on meditating on "Renewing the mind" truths.
- In the appendix, you will see a list of affirmations on renewing the mind.
- **Days 1-7** each day take the time to slowly read through 5 of the affirmations/scriptures.
- Next, you are going to speak these out loud.
- Take the affirmations/scriptures and ask the Lord to reveal to you how He wants you to apply these in your life.

Faith Actions

- What action of faith is the Lord asking you to do today? This could be praying a scripture prayer or speaking out some affirmations.
- Do your faith action 7 times a day.

Week Two Daily Plan (Days 8-14)

This week we will be renewing our minds on identity. This is very important as it is difficult to renew our minds effectively if we do not know who we are in Christ. Next week we will be addressing personal mountains and therefore this week is a great way to prepare. So take some time to pray and ask the Lord what He is asking you to renew your mind on from Week 3 onwards.

Quiet Time with the Lord

- Make sure you have your usual time with the Lord daily

Bible Study

- Read days 8-11 and complete the Bible study questions
- Days 12-14 speak all the daily affirmations & scripture prayers

Renewing the Mind Daily Suggestions

- Before you start, gather any materials or printables you are going to need

- Before you start mind renewal each day take a few moments in thanksgiving for what God is going to do in you as you renew your mind.

- At the end of each mind renewal session write down any revelations you received from the Lord in your personal journal or the mind renewal weekly tracker.

- Set the alarm for a minimum of 7 times a day ideally every hour and have armed with you scriptures that you are going to meditate on. You can also do your faith actions in these times.

- Before you go to bed take a scripture and meditate on this and see yourself in that scripture.

<u>Renewing the Mind Daily Plan – Week Two</u>

- This week we will be focusing on meditating on "Identity in Christ" truths
- In the appendix, you will see a list of affirmations & scriptures on identity.
- **Days 8-14** Each day take the time to read through 5 scriptures/affirmations slowly
- Next, you are going to speak these out loud
- Take the verses and ask the Lord to reveal to you how He wants you to apply THEM in your life

Faith Actions

- What action of faith is the Lord asking you to do today? This could be praying a scripture prayer or speaking out some affirmations.
- Do your faith action 7 times a day.

Week Three Daily Plan (Days 15-21)

This week, we will be tackling the "mountains" in our individual lives. A mountain is any obstacle to be removed as you seek to walk in spiritual victory. Choose an area in which you will continue to renew your mind for the remainder of this study. If you do not know what that is, take some time today to pray and ask the Lord what area He wants you to focus on.

Quiet Time with the Lord

- Make sure you have your usual time with the Lord daily

Bible Study

- Read days 15-17 and complete the Bible study questions
- Days 18-21 Speak all the daily affirmations & scripture prayers

Renewing the Mind Daily Plan

- Continue the below mind renewal plan daily

Renewing the Mind Daily Suggestions

- Before you start, gather any materials or printables you are going to need

- Before you start mind renewal each day take a few moments in thanksgiving for what God is going to do in you as you renew your mind.

- At the end of each mind renewal session write down any revelations you received from the Lord in your personal journal or the mind renewal weekly tracker.

- Set the alarm for a minimum of 7 times a day ideally every hour and have armed with you scriptures that you are going to meditate on. You can also do your faith actions in these times.

- Before you go to bed take a scripture and meditate on this and see yourself in that scripture.

Renewing the Mind Daily Plan – Week Three

***Day 15** We are going to practice prayer reading. Find 3-5 scriptures or a portion in the Bible that addresses your particular mountain and follow the steps in Day 15 on prayer reading. (You can also find some relevant scriptures in the appendix)

***Day 16** Let's renew our mind using scripture prayers. Take the scriptures you wrote on Day 15 and follow the How to steps on day 16 on scripture prayers in the study.

***Day 17** We are going to practice scripture journaling today. Please follow the steps on day 17 of the study.

***Day 18-21** Take all the truths in your journal & scripture prayers you received this week and meditate on these in your mind renewal time. Feel free to use more of the tools we learn this week

Faith Actions

- What action of faith is the Lord asking you to do today? This could be praying a scripture prayer or speaking out some affirmations.

Do your faith action 7 times a day.

Week Four Daily Plan (Days 22-28)

This week and the remainder of the study we will be tackling Mountains. Congratulations as you have now completed 21 days of renewing of the mind and you should be starting to see some changes in your thinking and behavior. Don't stop now; we need to keep going.

Quiet Time with the Lord

- Make sure you have your usual time with the Lord daily

Bible Study

- Read days 22-26 and complete the Bible study questions
- Days 27-28 Speak all the daily affirmations & scripture prayers

Renewing the Mind Daily Plan

- Continue the below mind renewal plan daily

Renewing the Mind Daily Suggestions

- Before you start, gather any materials or printables you are going to need

- Before you start mind renewal each day take a few moments in thanksgiving for what God is going to do in you as you renew your mind.

- At the end of each mind renewal session write down any revelations you received from the Lord in your personal journal or the mind renewal weekly tracker.

- Set the alarm for a minimum of 7 times a day ideally every hour and have armed with you scriptures that you are going to meditate on. You can also do your faith actions in these times.

- Before you go to bed take a scripture and meditate on this and see yourself in that scripture.

Renewing the Mind Daily Plan – Week Four

***Day 24** Today we are going to take the F.E.L.L.O.W.S.H.I.P prayers in the back of this book and start speaking these truths to yourself.

***Day 25** Today I want you to take some time to journal. Journal what your life is going to be like when this mountain is removed from your life. Praise God in expectation

***Day 26** Pick 2 key scriptures that you have been using to renew your mind with this week and practice repeating and emphasizing each word. Remember to be slow and intentional.

***Day 27- 28** Take all the truths in your journal & scripture prayers you received this week and meditate on these in your mind renewal time. You can also repeat any of the above tasks today.

Faith Actions
- What action of faith is the Lord asking you to do today? This could be, declaring your scripture cards, mirror exercise or praying the scripture prayers.
- Do your faith action 7 times a day.

Week Five Daily Plan (Days 29-35)

We are continuing with this journey. I am so excited for you and praying that you are being transformed daily. This week and next week we will be tackling our thought life and exchanging our thoughts for the thoughts of the mind of Christ. For the remainder of this study, let's add in 10 minutes before you sleep to meditate on the truths that God has revealed to you throughout the day.

Quiet Time with the Lord

- Make sure you have your usual time with the Lord daily

Bible Study

- Read days 29-31 and complete the Bible study questions
- Days 32-35 speak all the daily affirmations & scripture prayers

Renewing the Mind Daily Plan

- Continue the below mind renewal plan daily & 10 minutes review before you sleep.

Renewing the Mind Daily Suggestions

- Before you start, gather any materials or printables you are going to need

- Before you start mind renewal each day take a few moments in thanksgiving for what God is going to do in you as you renew your mind.

- At the end of each mind renewal session write down any revelations you received from the Lord in your personal journal or the mind renewal weekly tracker.

- Set the alarm for a minimum of 7 times a day ideally every hour and have armed with you scriptures that you are going to meditate on. You can also do your faith actions in these times.

- Before you go to bed take a scripture and meditate on this and see yourself in that scripture.

Renewing the Mind Daily Plan – Week Five

*Day 29 Today we are going to take some time and meditate on things above. Take the mountain you are demolishing and complete the Think On Model worksheet

*Day 30 Practice strengthening the God-given imagination the Lord has given you and practice the task on Day 30.

*Day 31 Today we are going to spend time talking to Holy Spirit about the mountain and the transformation so far and ask Him his views on the matter. Read day 31 to see the steps.

*Day 32- 35 Take all the truths in your journal & scripture prayers you received this week and meditate on these in your mind renewal time. You can also repeat any of the above tasks or from previous weeks on these days.

Faith Actions
- What action of faith is the Lord asking you to do today? This could be, declaring your scripture cards, mirror exercise or praying the scripture prayers.
- Do your faith action 7 times a day.

Week Six Daily Plan (Days 36-42)

We are now two thirds of the way through completing this study. This week we are going to be focusing on taking off lies and putting on truth, so we can line up with the mind of Christ.

Quiet Time with the Lord

- Make sure you have your usual time with the Lord daily

Bible Study

- Read days 36-39 and complete the Bible study questions
- Days 40-42 Speak all the daily affirmations & scripture prayers

Renewing the Mind Daily Plan

- Continue the below mind renewal plan daily & 10 minutes review before you sleep.

Renewing the Mind Daily Suggestions

- Before you start, gather any materials or printables you are going to need

- Before you start mind renewal each day take a few moments in thanksgiving for what God is going to do in you as you renew your mind.

- At the end of each mind renewal session write down any revelations you received from the Lord in your personal journal or the mind renewal weekly tracker.

- Set the alarm for a minimum of 7 times a day ideally every hour and have armed with you scriptures that you are going to meditate on. You can also do your faith actions in these times.

- Before you go to bed take a scripture and meditate on this and see yourself in that scripture.

Renewing the Mind Daily Plan – Week Six

*Day 36 Today we are going to practice meditating on God's Word again. Try talking to yourself about the scriptures and talk to Holy Spirit about the scriptures. You can also put your name in the appropriate places and speak them back to yourself. Choose scriptures that you have been leaning on over the past five weeks.

*Day 37 Practice strengthening the God-given imagination and practice the task on Day 30.

*Day 38 Today we are going to spend time being still and listening to what the Lord wants to say to you. Commit the last few weeks to Him and ask of Him what thoughts do you still need to deal with.

*Day 39 Let's spend some time taking thoughts captive and exchanging them for truth. Use the exercise from day 38

*Day 40- 42 Take all the truths in your journal & scripture prayers you received this week and meditate on these in your mind renewal time. You can also repeat any of the above tasks or from previous weeks on these days.

Faith Actions
- What action of faith is the Lord asking you to do today? This could be, declaring your scripture cards, mirror exercise or praying the scripture prayers.
- Do your faith action 7 times a day.

Week Seven Daily Plan (Days 43-49)

Over the next two weeks, we want to start cementing what we have learned so far and ensured we have key practices and tools in place to ensure we finish well.

Quiet Time with the Lord
- Make sure you have your usual time with the Lord daily

Bible Study
- Read days 43-45 and complete the Bible study questions
- Days 46-49 Speak all the daily affirmations & scripture prayers

Renewing the Mind Daily Plan
- Continue the below mind renewal plan daily & 10 minutes review before you sleep.

Renewing the Mind Daily Suggestions

- Before you start, gather any materials or printables you are going to need

- Before you start mind renewal each day take a few moments in thanksgiving for what God is going to do in you as you renew your mind.

- At the end of each mind renewal session write down any revelations you received from the Lord in your personal journal or the mind renewal weekly tracker.

- Set the alarm for a minimum of 7 times a day ideally every hour and have armed with you scriptures that you are going to meditate on. You can also do your faith actions in these times.

- Before you go to bed take a scripture and meditate on this and see yourself in that scripture.

Renewing the Mind Daily Plan – Week Seven

*Day 43 Today pick a renewing of the mind tool that you sense is the best for you today

*Day 44 Let's use the Think On Model again today to focus on all you have achieved these past weeks

*Day 45 Complete a session of repeating and emphasizing 1 or 2 key scriptures based on the mountain you have been working on.

*Day 46 Look back over your journal entry on what your life will look back when you are transformed and spend time praising God and seeing yourself in that place

*Day 47- 49 Take all the truths in your journal & scripture prayers you received this week and meditate on these in your mind renewal time. You can also repeat any of the above tasks or from previous weeks on these days.

Faith Actions
- What action of faith is the Lord asking you to do today? This could be, declaring your scripture cards, mirror exercise or praying the scripture prayers.
- Do your faith action 7 times a day.

Week Eight Daily Plan (Days 50-56)

Praise God for all the mighty work he has been doing in you. This week we talk about time management, setting goals and boundaries. Take some time this week in your spare time to download the goals worksheet on www.sophiatucker.com and think about future goals for renewing the mind and other areas of life going forward.

Quiet Time with the Lord
- Make sure you have your usual time with the Lord daily

Bible Study
- Read days 50-53 and complete the Bible study questions
- Days 54-56 Speak all the daily affirmations & scripture prayers

Renewing the Mind Daily Plan
- Continue the below mind renewal plan daily & 10 minutes review before you sleep.

Renewing the Mind Daily Suggestions

- Before you start, gather any materials or printables you are going to need

- Before you start mind renewal each day take a few moments in thanksgiving for what God is going to do in you as you renew your mind.

- At the end of each mind renewal session write down any revelations you received from the Lord in your personal journal or the mind renewal weekly tracker.

- Set the alarm for a minimum of 7 times a day ideally every hour and have armed with you scriptures that you are going to meditate on. You can also do your faith actions in these times.

- Before you go to bed take a scripture and meditate on this and see yourself in that scripture.

Renewing the Mind Daily Plan – Eight

*Day 51 Let's write out some more scripture prayers today based on 2-3 scriptures

*Day 52 Complete a session of repeating and emphasizing 1 or 2 critical scriptures based on the mountain you have been working on.

*Day 53 Talk to Holy Spirit today about what He thinks, see's and feels about your journey thus far.

*Day 54- 56 Take all the truths in your journal & scripture prayers you received this week and meditate on these in your mind renewal time. You can also repeat any of the above tasks or from previous weeks on these days.

Faith Actions
- What action of faith is the Lord asking you to do today? This could be, declaring your scripture cards, mirror exercise or praying the scripture prayers.
- Do your faith action 7 times a day.

Week Nine Daily Plan (Days 57-63)

Friend you have now reached the final week of this study! CONGRATULATIONS! Now, this week I want you to take the reins more and take the time to choose the methods of mind renewal you want to do each day. Please write in your journal this week all the changes that have happened over these last nine weeks.

If you feel like the mountain is still holding on a little take more time to ensure you renew your mind by focusing on truths you have discovered over the last nine weeks. Again praise the Lord for this journey.

Quiet Time with the Lord
- Make sure you have your usual time with the Lord daily

Bible Study
- Read days 57-59 and complete the Bible study questions
- Days 60-63 Speak all the daily affirmations & scripture prayers

Renewing the Mind Daily Plan
- Continue the below mind renewal plan daily & 10 minutes review before you sleep.

Renewing the Mind Daily Suggestions

- Before you start, gather any materials or printables you are going to need

- Before you start mind renewal each day take a few moments in thanksgiving for what God is going to do in you as you renew your mind.

- At the end of each mind renewal session write down any revelations you received from the Lord in your personal journal or the mind renewal weekly tracker.

- Set the alarm for a minimum of 7 times a day ideally every hour and have armed with you scriptures that you are going to meditate on. You can also do your faith actions in these times.

- Before you go to bed take a scripture and meditate on this and see yourself in that scripture.

Renewing the Mind Daily Plan – Nine

*Day 57 – 63 Take the time to practice using the most beneficial tools for mind renewal for you each day.

*Ask the Lord what He wants you to implement after this study.

Faith Actions

- What action of faith is the Lord asking you to do today? This could be declaring your scripture cards, mirror exercise or praying the scripture prayer. Whatever you choose make sure it is just 1 minute long and write it down in your journal or the accountability worksheet and move to step 5

SCRIPTURE VERSES

Find on the following pages a list of non-exhaustive scriptures relating to principal mountains and areas you may be renewing our minds on.

Bible Verses on renewing the mind

Romans 12:2 - And be not conformed to this world: but be ye transformed by the renewing of your mind, that ye may prove what [is] that good, and acceptable, and perfect, will of God.

Philippians 4:8 - Finally, brethren, whatsoever things are true, whatsoever things [are] honest, whatsoever things [are] just, whatsoever things [are] pure, whatsoever things [are] lovely, whatsoever things [are] of good report; if [there be] any virtue, and if [there be] any praise, think on these things.

Romans 12:1-2 - I beseech you, therefore, brethren, by the mercies of God, that ye present your bodies a living sacrifice, holy, acceptable unto God, [which is] your reasonable service. And be not conformed to this world: but be ye transformed by the renewing of your mind, that ye may prove what [is] that good, and acceptable, and perfect, will of God.

2 Corinthians 4:16 - For which cause we faint not; but though our outward man perish, yet the inward [man] is renewed day by day.

Philippians 4:6-7 - Be careful for nothing, but in everything by prayer and supplication with thanksgiving let your requests be made known unto God. 7 And the peace of God, which passeth all understanding, shall keep your hearts and minds through Christ Jesus.

Psalms 119:11 - Thy word have I hid in mine heart, that I might not sin against thee.

Ephesians 4:23 - And be renewed in the spirit of your mind;

1 Peter 1:13 - Wherefore gird up the loins of your mind, be sober, and hope to the end for the grace that is to be brought unto you at the revelation of Jesus Christ;

2 Corinthians 10:4-5 - (For the weapons of our warfare [are] not carnal, but mighty through God to the pulling down of strong holds;) Casting down imaginations, and every high thing that exalteth itself against the knowledge of God, and bringing into captivity every thought to the obedience of Christ;

Colossians 3:2 - Set your affection on things above, not on things on the earth.

John 8:32 - And ye shall know the truth, and the truth shall make you free.

Colossians 3:16 - Let the word of Christ dwell in you richly in all wisdom; teaching and admonishing one another in psalms and hymns and spiritual songs, singing with grace in your hearts to the Lord.

Philippians 2:5 - Let this mind be in you, which was also in Christ Jesus:

Jeremiah 29:11 - For I know the thoughts that I think toward you, saith the LORD, thoughts of peace, and not of evil, to give you an expected end.

Ephesians 4:20-24 - But ye have not so learned Christ; 21 If so be that ye have heard him, and have been taught by him, as the truth is in Jesus:22 That ye put off concerning the former conversation the old man, which is corrupt according to the deceitful lusts;23 And be renewed in the spirit of your mind; 24 And that ye put on the new man, which after God is created in righteousness and true holiness.

John 17:17 - Sanctify them through thy truth: thy word is truth.

Isaiah 40:31 - But they that wait upon the LORD shall renew [their] strength; they shall mount up with wings as eagles; they shall run, and not be weary; [and] they shall walk, and not faint.

1 Corinthians 2:16 - For who hath known the mind of the Lord, that he may instruct him? But we have the mind of Christ.

Bible Verses on Identity

2 Corinthians 5:17 – Therefore, if anyone is in Christ, he is a new creation. The old has passed away; behold, the new has come.

1 Peter 2:9 – But you are a chosen race, a royal priesthood, a holy nation, a people for his own possession, that you may proclaim the excellencies of him who called you out of darkness into his marvellous light.

Galatians 2:20 – I have been crucified with Christ. It is no longer I who live, but Christ who lives in me. And the life I now live in the flesh I live by faith in the Son of God, who loved me and gave himself for me.

John 15:15 – No longer do I call you servants, for the servant, does not know what his master is doing; but I have called you friends, for all that I have heard from my Father I have made known to you.

John 1:12 – But to all who did receive him, who believed in his name, he gave the right to become children of God.

Romans 8:17 – And if children, then heirs—heirs of God and fellow heirs with Christ, provided we suffer with him in order that we may also be glorified with him.

Colossians 3:3 – For you have died, and your life is hidden with Christ in God.

Galatians 3:26 – For in Christ Jesus you are all sons of God, through faith.

Romans 8:1 – There is therefore now no condemnation for those who are in Christ Jesus.

Philippians 3:20 – But our citizenship is in heaven, and from it, we await a Saviour, the Lord Jesus Christ.

1 Corinthians 12:27 – Now you are the body of Christ and individually members of it.

1 Corinthians 6:19-20 – Or do you not know that your body is a temple of the Holy Spirit within you, whom you have from God? You are not your own, for you were bought with a price. So glorify God in your body.

Ephesians 2:10 – For we are God's masterpiece, created to do good works which God prepared in advance for us to do.

Ephesians 4:24 – And to put on the new self, created after the likeness of God in true righteousness and holiness.

John 3:16 – For God so loved the world, that he gave his only Son, that whoever believes in him should not perish but have eternal life.

Bible Verses on Fear

Fear thou not; for I am with thee:
be not dismayed; for I am thy God:
I will strengthen thee; yea, I will help thee;
yea, I will uphold thee with the right hand of my righteousness.
Isaiah 41:10

What time I am afraid, I will trust in thee.
Psalm 56:3

Have not I commanded thee? Be strong and of a good courage; be not afraid, neither be thou dismayed: for the Lord thy God is with thee whithersoever thou goest.
Joshua 1:9

Be careful for nothing; but in everything by prayer and supplication with thanksgiving let your requests be made known unto God. And the peace of God, which passeth all understanding, shall keep your hearts and minds through Christ Jesus.
Philippians 4:6-7

For I the Lord thy God
will hold thy right hand,
saying unto thee, Fear not;
I will help thee.
Isaiah 41:13 | KJV

The Lord is on my side; I will not fear:
what can man do unto me?
Psalm 118:6 | KJV

There is no fear in love; but perfect love casteth out fear: because
fear hath torment. He that feareth is not made perfect in love.
1 John 4:18 | KJV

Yea, though I walk
through the valley of the shadow of death,
I will fear no evil:
for thou art with me;
thy rod and thy staff they comfort me.
Psalm 23:4 | KJV

Bible Verses on Love (These verses are in NIV)

Love is patient; love is kind. It does not envy; it does not boast; it is
not proud. It does not dishonour others; it is not self-seeking; it is
not easily angered; it keeps no record of wrongs.
1 Corinthians 13:4-5 | NIV

Do everything in love.
1 Corinthians 16:14 | NIV

Let the morning bring me word of your unfailing love,
for I have put my trust in you.
Show me the way I should go,
for to you I entrust my life.
Psalm 143:8 | NIV

Let love and faithfulness never leave you;
bind them around your neck,
write them on the tablet of your heart.
Then you will win favour and a good name
in the sight of God and man.
Proverbs 3:3-4 | NIV

And over all these virtues put on love, which binds them all together
in perfect unity.
Colossians 3:14 | NIV

And so we know and rely on the love God has for us. God is love.
Whoever lives in love lives in God, and God in them.
1 John 4:16 | NIV

Be completely humble and gentle; be patient, bearing with one another in love.
Ephesians 4:2 | NIV

We love because He first loved us.
1 John 4:19 | NIV

And now these three remain faith, hope, and love. But the greatest of these is love.
1 Corinthians 13:13 | NIV

Above all, love each other deeply, because love covers over a multitude of sins.
1 Peter 4:8 | NIV

I pray that out of his glorious riches he may strengthen you with power through his Spirit in your inner being, so that Christ may dwell in your hearts through faith. And I pray that you, being rooted and established in love.
Ephesians 3:16-17 | NIV

Love must be sincere. Hate what is evil; cling to what is good.
Romans 12:9 | NIV

If I have the gift of prophecy and can fathom all mysteries and all knowledge, and if I have a faith that can move mountains, but do not have love, I am nothing.
Corinthians 13:2 | NIV

Bible verses on Neighbours/Friends/Family (KJV)

And the second is like, namely this, Thou shalt love thy neighbour as thyself. There is none other commandment greater than these.
Mark 12:31 | KJV

Finally, be ye all of one mind, having compassion one of another, love as brethren, be pitiful, be courteous.
1 Peter 3:8 | KJV

Wherefore comfort yourselves together, and edify one another, even as also ye do.
1 Thessalonians 5:11 | KJV

Let no man seek his own, but every man another's wealth.
1 Corinthians 10:24 | KJV

Bear ye one another's burdens, and so fulfil the law of Christ.
Galatians 6:2 | KJV

For all the law is fulfilled in one word, even in this; Thou shalt love thy neighbour as thyself.
Galatians 5:14 | KJV

Let brotherly love continue. Be not forgetful to entertain strangers: for thereby some have entertained angels unawares.
Hebrews 13:1-2 | KJV

Therefore all things whatsoever ye would that men should do to you, do ye even so to them: for this is the law and the prophets.
Matthew 7:12 | KJV

Let nothing be done through strife or vainglory, but in lowliness of mind let each esteem other better than themselves.
Philippians 2:3 | KJV

Bible Verses on Humility

Be completely humble and gentle; be patient, bearing with one another in love.
Ephesians 4:2 | NIV

Do nothing out of selfish ambition or vain conceit. Rather, in humility value others above yourselves.
Philippians 2:3 | NIV

When pride comes, then comes disgrace,
but with humility comes wisdom.
Proverbs 11:2 | NIV

Live in harmony with one another. Do not be proud, but be willing to associate with people of low position. Do not be conceited.
Romans 12:16 | NIV

Humble yourselves before the Lord, and he will lift you up.
James 4:10 | NIV

Your beauty should not come from outward adornment, such as elaborate hairstyles and the wearing of gold jewellery or fine clothes. Rather, it should be that of your inner self, the unfading beauty of a gentle and quiet spirit, which is of great worth in God's sight.
1 Peter 3:3-4 | NIV

Therefore, as God's chosen people, holy and dearly loved, clothe yourselves with compassion, kindness, humility, gentleness, and patience.
Colossians 3:12 | NIV

Pride brings a person low,
but the lowly in spirit gain honour.
Proverbs 29:23 | NIV

Humility is the fear of the Lord;
its wages are riches and honour and life.
Proverbs 22:4 | NIV

Humble yourselves, therefore, under God's mighty hand, that he may lift you up in due time.
1 Peter 5:6 | NIV

If my people, who are called by my name, will humble themselves and pray and seek my face and turn from their wicked ways, then I will hear from heaven, and I will forgive their sin and will heal their land.
2 Chronicles 7:14 | NIV

Bible Verses on Wisdom (NIV)

For the Lord gives wisdom;
from his mouth come knowledge and understanding.
Proverbs 2:6 | NIV

Be very careful, then, how you live—not as unwise but as wise, making the most of every opportunity, because the days are evil.
Ephesians 5:15-16 | NIV

If any of you lacks wisdom, you should ask God, who gives generously to all without finding fault, and it will be given to you.
James 1:5 | NIV

But the wisdom that comes from heaven is first of all pure; then peace-loving, considerate, submissive, full of mercy and good fruit, impartial and sincere.
James 3:17 | NIV

How much better to get wisdom than gold,
to get insight rather than silver!
Proverbs 16:16 | NIV

Do not say, "Why were the old days better than these?"
For it is not wise to ask such questions.
Ecclesiastes 7:10 | NIV

Be wise in the way you act toward outsiders; make the most of every opportunity. Let your conversation be always full of grace, seasoned with salt, so that you may know how to answer everyone.
Colossians 4:5-6 | NIV

Where there is strife, there is pride,
but wisdom is found in those who take advice.
Proverbs 13:10 | NIV

The one who gets wisdom loves life;
the one who cherishes understanding will soon prosper.
Proverbs 19:8 | NIV

Do not deceive yourselves. If any of you think you are wise by the standards of this age, you should become "fools" so that you may become wise.
1 Corinthians 3:18 | NIV

Those who guard their lips preserve their lives,
but those who speak rashly will come to ruin.
Proverbs 13:3 | NIV

AFFIRMATIONS

Identity Affirmations

Thank you, Lord that you look at the depths of heart and not only the external works. I submit my heart openly to your leadership in my life.

I am one minded with you and can know your mind as I have the mind of Christ and we can know your ways, and know what to do in every situation.

I am the temple of the Living God, and You take delight in me and who I am. It is your enjoyment to commune with me.

God and I are divinely connected. I belong to Him, and He accepts me as His own.

You wrap me in your arms no matter the circumstances I face; You love me with love like no other. With everlasting love and faithfulness, you draw me to yourself.

Father, you long to commune with me, you extend your loving kindness to me.

Thank you that you dwell inside me and you are within the midst of my heart. You are mighty, Saviour and hallelujah redeemer.

You make no mention of past sins, and I refuse to meditate on these. But you sing over me with rejoicing.

I am of great worth! Not forgotten/forsaken and in right standing with God.

The word says I am God's handiwork and He has predestined me for good works. This means that I can do the work you have called me to do and everything you have called to be.

The Lord has prepared my paths ahead of time. I do not fret nor do I worry.

I am a chosen woman/man of God chosen to display the wonderful beauty of God in every endeavor.

I expect that I will be strengthened in might to continue in this journey, which will aid every part of my body, soul, mind, and heart.

I shall not be known after the flesh but my Spirit. I refer to my spirit and not my efforts, abilities nor circumstances.

Hallelujah Christ alone is the Rock of which I stand all else is sinking sand.

I am called out of the darkness and into the light. Hallelujah

The Love of God Affirmations

Perfect love is casting out all fear in my life. I am casting out those boats of fears into the ocean. I choose to let go of the ropes. Jesus, you hold me.

I am fully infused with Holy Spirit who connects, roots and grounds me in the heart of the Father which is total love, therefore, Christ dwells in my heart.

I am daily engulfed, filled and flooded with the love of God. It casts out anything else that should not be there.

Holy Spirit enables me and teaches me and leads me in love.

I ask of the Holy Spirit all day what He thinks about all things, and He counsels me.

Now I can see, hear and feel the love of the Father in all circumstances as His love surpasses all knowledge of fear.

The width, height, length, and depth of His love is the cross personified. His love goes as deep, high, wide and long as the entire universe's a trillion times over.

The love of the work of the cross means I am fully complete and whole.

I am secure in the grounding of the Father's love.

I am personally experiencing the love of God; therefore, I look through His eyes at every situation with total peace.

I have been, and I am continually being strengthened and energized with Gods power through His Spirit into my very being.

I am deeply rooted and secure in God's love

I can understand the width and length and height and depth of His love by fully experiencing that amazing and endless love.

The Love of God surpasses all mere knowledge and logic.

My heart will continue to grow in love more and more and more. Thank you Holy Spirit for showing me things I am holding onto, and that need releasing.

I love all. I love God with all my heart, soul and strength. I love all people as I love myself.

The love of God has been put into my heart, therefore I walk in love, and I do not hold anything against anyone.

The peace of God Affirmations

I have peace, not as the world gives: Christ has left me his peace. The peace he has given to me and not the peace that the world gives. Thus, I do not let my heart be troubled, or let it be fearful.

Christ overcame the world: Through my union with Christ, I have peace through the things that He has spoken to me. In the world I will encounter oppression, but I take courage because Christ has overcome the world.

Let the peace of God rule: I let the peace of God rule in my heart since I was called in one body to peace with thankfulness.

No stumbling: I have great peace because I love God's law. Nothing causes me to stumble. Psalms 119:165

Father, You are the source of perfect peace: You will keep me in perfect peace because my mind is fixed on you; because I place my confidence in you. Isaiah 26:3

Guarded by the Peace of God: Because I override anxiety by taking every issue and request to God through prayer and petition with thanksgiving; therefore the peace of God, which surpasses all understanding, guards my heart and my mind through Christ Jesus. Philippians 4:6, 7

Peace is like a river: You are the Lord my Redeemer, the Holy One of Israel: the Lord my God, who teaches me to profit, who leads me by the way that I should go. Because I have followed to your commands, I have peace like a river, and righteousness as the waves of the sea Isaiah 58:17, 18

I sleep in peace: In peace, I will lay myself down and sleep, for you, Lord alone, make me live in safety. Psalms 4:8

I embrace the mind of the Spirit: For the mind of the flesh is death, but the mind of the Spirit is life and peace; I'm not in the flesh but the Spirit, because the Spirit of God dwells in me. Romans 8:6, 8

Peace, healing and truth: You Lord bring us health and healing; you reveal to us an abundance of peace and truth. Jeremiah 33:6

Filled with all joy and peace: Now the God of hope fills me with all joy and peace as I exercise my faith, so that I will abound in hope, through the power of the Holy Spirit. Romans 15:13

His covenant of peace shall not be removed: The Lord who has mercy on me has promised that even if the mountains should depart, and the hills are removed yet His loving kindness shall not depart from me neither shall His covenant of peace be removed. Isaiah 54:10

Lord you have great plans and thoughts for me, they are plans of peace. I walk in that peace today.

Hope & Perseverance
Affirmations

I may not know the exact specifics over the future, but I stand in confidence in You my God and who You are. I shall not miss the in the meantime seasons as they build greatly in our lives, marriage, and children. Your timing is perfect. I don't mind waiting.

Every promise You have made I stand strong in them and in the overflow of confidence I stand in peace and strength.

Today I will focus and keep moving forward and upwards from glory to glory not looking back, not entertaining thoughts of mine or others that are contrary to Your promises.

I am focusing on the journey to the end and destination of each thing of my life with joy and excitement and praise. I will walk in contentment as each season is for a reason.

I relinquish all abilities to be moved as my hope and provision is in Christ.

My hope is in YOU Lord. Holy Spirit I believe that you move powerfully through me in Hope right now.

You are my strength, strong Tower and the mighty stronghold in me.

I do not fear the future, money or balance in my life as God has the perfect plan for us and I choose to trust You and will not worry about everything.

I look forward to growth and to any discomfort that this growth may bring. I believe that resistance provides strength.

I die to my flesh that is trying to figure all things out. My future is SECURE AND FAVOURED AND PROSPERED IN EVERYTHING I DO.

God is my stronghold. I am never alone and never forsaken.

I am running my race in faithfulness. Jesus Christ and the cloud of witnesses are surrounding me watching. I am running a race with Christ, so I strip off every unnecessary weight and sin.

I walk on water today, no capsizing, no head barely above the waters of my life EVER!!!

I have set the Lord continually before me; Because He is at my right hand, I will not be shaken.

Loving Others
Affirmations

I will serve my family, friends, and others unselfishly today in joy and strength and energy from resting in love with You. I can do all things through Christ who strengthens me.

The mountain of people pleasing shall be brought low today. People will see Christ in me as it is Him who lives and not me.

I do not condemn myself or receive condemnation by others. I will not walk in fear, for You are for me, who and what can be against me.

I am united with Christ now. You will give me authority when to speak up in defense. In the meantime, I trust who I am in Christ and take no offense to the opinions or actions of others.

I freely release others. Holding no bitterness or resentment and focus on all the good in them and hoping for the best for them.

I will not speak negatively about anyone only speaking edification to the listener to build them up.

I do not fear confrontation knowing I walk by the Spirit and every response is undergirded by love. I look and hope in expectation for good love outcomes.

I shall not allow myself to respond in anger or fear. But in all my ways acknowledge You Lord as my peace as I lay down my life.

Healing Affirmations

My body has been designed perfectly by the skilled hands of the master creator and knows what is best for optimum efficiency. I trust the manufacturer of my body.

My heart is glad, and my glory [my inner being] rejoices, and my body too will dwell [confidently] in safety,

I sleep in peace. I do not fear sleep; it is a great training tool, and You teach me in my night watches. You will give your beloved (that's me) rest.

You are closer to me than every organ in my body. Your Word is powerful to pierce between soul and spirit. Therefore I shall not worry as You will lift me up and cause me to be strong.

I stand and believe God for my healing. You will give me the strength to endure with promise.

I know that it is your will that I will be in health and prosper as my soul prospers.

I receive prosperity in my heart in my soul in my mind and my body.

Your Word is my medicine because it is Spirt and it is life to me.

Many times Jesus healed them all, proving that it is always Your will for me to be healed. I receive Your healing Word for my situation now.

One of your names is I am the Lord your God that heals you, Father God you never change, You are the same for me today, now faith is my substance that I am hoping for, I receive now faith, as I receive your now word for me, your word heals and blesses me now.

Renewing the Mind & The Word

Affirmations

Today I walk in the fear the LORD and serve him faithfully with all my heart. I will meditate and consider what great things He has done for me.

The truth of your Word and peace flows through my whole being like a river. And every area of my life is richly vegetated by the sustenance of peace that comes from that river.

My true foundation is on the stable ground of Christ. The mighty rock that I stand ON is Him, His word, obeying His commands and abiding in His presence.

I have a God centered mind, and I have a sound and stable mind being renewed daily.

I have the mind of Christ dwelling in me. I have this because I am born again. I am a new creature, in Christ. Hallelujah old things have passed away, and all things have become new.

I am partnering with the Holy Spirit who is going a deep inner working in me.

I am renewing my mind and pulling up those weeds of toxic thoughts in my mind. It may feel messy and uncomfortable, but I have to get my hands in.

This work that God is doing in me is because I asked to know how to renew my mind. I labor to enter into the rest God set for me

I call on you today Lord, I come to pray to you, and I can hear your voice and You listen to me.

With a deep longing, I seek you today, and I require of You today. It is of vital necessity as I search You with all my heart.

I look away from everything that distracts me and keeps my eyes fixed on Jesus. Hallelujah He is the Author and Finisher of my faith.

I will bless the Lord who has counseled me; indeed, my heart (mind) instructs me in the night.

TRUE warfare is that I take every thought captive. IT IS NOT A CHOICE. THIS IS WHERE THE BATTLE IS. I will take all THE THOUGHTS CAPTIVE to the obedience of Christ.

I choose to keep AND set my mind fully and firmly centered on Christ and heavenly things by walking continuously in communion with Holy Spirit living out the fruit of the Spirit.

I choose not to focus on matters pertaining to this worldly system but focus on matters of the kingdom, for I have died to this world and its temporal fascinations.

I am putting to death and depriving the flesh of its desires. And anything that gets in the way of my full devotions to God.

If I am feeling anxious, I lay down relax and ask Holy Spirit to show me the toxic thought and how to pull down. I write down what the Lord will show me.

I shall be anxious for nothing. I shall not be moved by the things I have to do today.

I stand in praise and thanksgiving while utterly CASTING AND THROWING DOWN my cares at Your feet. Then I SHALL teach this to others.

The Word is the final authority in my life. God said it, I believe it. It is settled in my life.

You have not given me a spirit of timidity or fear. I have the mind of Christ which is full of power and love and full of sound judgment.

With the mind of Christ, I can walk in personal discipline, calmness, balance, and self-control.

I declare Your peace stands as a strong guardsman over the gate of my heart and surrounds my mind. Nothing can enter.

Thank you, lord that any issues I have experienced have been through a lack of knowledge of understanding of how to pull down thoughts and taking them captive. I praise you that you have now given and are giving me a master class in renewing my mind today.

My mind is renewed. My thoughts are pure and of good report. I think on things that are pure and if good report, things that bring joy to God and peace to my spirit.

SCRIPTURE PRAYERS

Identity

Who you are in Christ

Father, I thank you that I can say boldly that I am in Christ, and I have become an entirely new creation. The old has vanished, and I rejoice because everything is fresh and new. My life is empowered with the Spirit of Christ; I am not dominated by the flesh any longer; I am led by the spirit. I am joined to the Spirit of the Anointed One, I am joined with Christ.

2 Corinthians 5:17, Romans 8:9

You are my God of peace and harmony; you have set me apart, making me completely holy. I pray that my entire being—spirit, soul, and body—be kept completely flawless until the coming of our Lord Jesus, the Anointed One.

1 Thessalonians 5:23

Father, I thank you for giving me the living Word. It is full of divine living energy and power, and it pierces me more sharply than any two-edged sword. It penetrates to the very core of my being dividing soulish-ness and spirituality, bone and marrow, cleaning my blood, my DNA and my past! It enables me to interpret and reveal my true thoughts and the secret motives of my heart, for no one else can see these except for my spirit, just as no one can see Your thoughts except for the Spirit of God. I thank you that I have not received the spirit of the World, but I have received the Holy Spirit from You. Now I can know and understand the wonderful things You have freely given to me. Hallelujah!

Hebrews 4:12, 1 Corinthians 2:11-12

Father, I thank you that Your Spirit leads me, I confidently accept the revelations that you have hidden in Christ for me to discover joyfully. Because I have Your Spirit living in me, I can discern your revelations, receive them and experience the reality of them in my life. Thank you Holy Spirit, you are wonderful.

1 Corinthians 2:14

Father, I cast off the old sinful nature, which was never your will for me anyway. I do not belong to this world any longer; I am a citizen of heaven. I am led by the Holy Spirit and have set aside all jealousy and quarrelsome attitudes. I have learned to walk in your spirit and have found maturity in Christ.

Corinthians 3:1-3

I thank you, Father God, for the wisdom from above, as it is first of all pure, because of it I am peace loving, gentle at all times, and willing to yield to others. I am full of mercy and the fruit of good deeds. I show no favoritism and I am always sincere. I thank you for making me a peacemaker and giving me the opportunity to plant seeds of peace and reap a harvest of righteousness.

James 3:13-18

I thank You, Father that I do not walk as a natural man any longer but I am a spirit and a child of the Highest. I can hear your truths and judge righteously. The natural man cannot know the mind of the Lord but my old man is dead, and I have the mind of Christ. I can understand all your ways. In Jesus' name, Amen

1 Corinthians 2:14-16

Father, I thank you for the wisdom to understand all of your ways. I receive the fruit of wisdom as I live my life in an honorable way, doing good works with humility. I ask you to reveal any bitter jealousy or selfish ambition that may be left in my heart. I don't want to cover up the truth with boasting or lying. For jealousy and selfishness are not Your kinds of wisdom. I declare before You

Father that I renounce everything that is, unspiritual and demonic, I am not earthly, I am heavenly. I am only jealous for more of who you are and your glory to be revealed in and through me, nothing else is worth my jealousy! My ambition is to serve Jesus and His will on earth with all that is within me. Father, I give you permission to order my steps completely.

Dear Father, I want all my works to be done full of the wisdom that comes from You. I refuse fleshly and earthly wisdom, which isn't wisdom at all. Remove any envy and self-seeking from my heart, including any confusion, as I know, these are signs that I need to grow in walking in heavenly wisdom. Help me cling to the true wisdom available to me that it is pure, peaceful, gentle and willing to yield. This kind of wisdom belongs to me as it lives in my spirit; increase your work in me. To Jesus my King I surrender all.

The Mind of Christ

Father, my deepest desire is to satisfy you, I believe in Jesus, the one you sent to save me. I can say confidently that I have the mind of Christ and hold the thoughts, feelings, and purposes of His heart.

John 6:28-29, 1 Corinthians 2:16

Jesus, teach me to have the same attitude that you have. Though you are God, when you walked the earth you did not think of equality with God as some cling to. You gave up your divine privileges, took the humble position of a servant. Through your example of being a living sacrifice, I have gained spiritual maturity and hold onto these convictions, I will follow Your ways and emulate You, so will I be Your disciple.

Philippians 2:5-7, Philippians 3:15

Father, today I chose life. I choose to keep and obey your commandments, to love you and walk in Your ways. I believe your words are for me when you tell me that; I will live a blessed life of multiplication and that I will be blessed in the land that I have possessed.

Deuteronomy 30:15-16

What does the Mind of Christ look like?

Father, I thank you that you have given me the mind of Christ. I thank you that I can ask for anything in prayer, in accordance with Your will, I believe with confident trust that I have received the mind of Christ, and with Christ, I receive every good thing.

Luke 8:30, Matthew 8:16, Mark 11:20-24

Jesus, since I am now joined to You, I have been given the treasures of redemption by Your blood—the total cancellation of my sins—all because of the cascading riches of Your grace. Through your grace, I can forgive others fully and completely. I am able to enter the throne room of grace because my relationship with God is not hindered by hurt or anger. I am completely forgiven.

Ephesians 1:7 Matthew 6:15

Biblical Affirmation

Father, I thank you that the same spirit of faith that is described in the scripture is now in me. I know I must first believe and then speak in faith and I convinced that You who raised Jesus will raise me up as well. I live and move and have my being in Your presence; I am Your offspring.

2 Corinthians 4:13-14 Acts 17:29

Father, thank you for giving me words wisdom so that I may share them and find is satisfaction in my inner being. It encourages me to know that through You I've changed someone else's life. Keep giving me the understanding that my words are so powerful that they hold the power of life and death. I choose life so that I and others may find life and prosper in You.

Proverbs 18:20-21

Spiritual Battle

Father, I thank you for the revelation that for although I live in the natural realm, I don't wage a military campaign employing human weapons, using manipulation to achieve my aims. Instead, my spiritual weapons are energized with divine power to dismantle strongholds effectively. I can demolish every deceptive imagination that opposes God and break through every arrogant attitude that is raised up in defiance of Your true knowledge. I capture, like prisoners of war, every thought and insist that it bow in obedience to Jesus Christ.
2 Corinthians 10:3-5

Thank you, Father, for your wonderful mercies! I receive your word of power. I receive your wisdom; I receive the mystery of Christ in me which was hidden before time itself. Oh, how wonderful to know that you thought of me before the world, you finished your works and planned that I would come to know you through Jesus. I have received the Spirit of God. I receive everything I need freely from God. I am therefore equipped to win in every area of my life. I thank you that you take joy in me as I move forward and claim everything you have prepared for me. Thank you, Father, in Jesus' name, Amen.

1 Corinthians 2:4-12

Spending time in His presence

Father God, thank you for the Word that lives in me richly and flooding me with all wisdom. Continue to show me how to apply the Scriptures as I teach and instruct others with the Psalms, and with festive praises, and with prophetic songs given to me spontaneously by the Spirit, I sing to God with all my heart!

Colossians 3:16

Father, I have confidence and great boldness that I can come before You and ask anything according to Your will. You will hear me. And You will continually revitalize me, implanting within me the passion for doing what pleases You. Because I live my life in union with You and Your words live powerfully within me—I know I can ask whatever I desire and it will be done.

1 John 5:14 , Philippians 2:13, John 15:7

Prayer Reading

Thank you, God, that I have love, and I remain in faith and hope. Thank you, Father, that above all your love resides in me, I focus on your love Father

1 Corinthians 13:13

Scripture Journaling

Father, thank you for giving me the living Word of God, which is full of living power, like a two-edged sword. It penetrates to the very core of my being where my soul, spirit, bone, and marrow meet! It interprets and reveals my true thoughts and secret motives of my heart."
Hebrews 4:12

Father, thank you for the authority to demolish every deceptive belief system and fantasy that opposes You and that I am able to break through every arrogant attitude that is raised up in defiance of Your true knowledge. I capture, like prisoners of war, every thought and insist that it bow in obedience to Jesus the Anointed One. I am armed with dynamic weaponry; I stand ready to punish any trace of rebellion, as soon as I choose complete obedience."
2 Corinthians 10:5-6

Managing Time

Holy Spirit, remind me to be very careful of how I live, not being like those with no understanding, but I choose to live honorably with true wisdom, for I am living in evil times. I take full advantage of every day as I spend my life for Your purpose. And because I don't live foolishly, I have the discernment to understand Your will fully."
Ephesians 5:15-17

Think on these things

Father, I keep my thoughts continually fixed on all that is authentic and real, honorable and admirable, beautiful and respectful, pure and holy, merciful and kind. I fasten my thoughts on Your glorious work, praising You always.

Philippians 4:8

Repeat & Emphasise Scripture

Father, I found Your words, and I ate them, and your words became to me a joy and the delight of my heart, for I am called by your name, O Lord, God of hosts. And I have discovered that bread alone will not satisfy, but true life is found in every word, which constantly goes forth from Your mouth. How sweet are your living promises to me; sweeter than honey is your revelation-light.

Jeremiah 15:16, Matthew 4:4, Psalms 119:103

Meditation

Father, What a delight it is to follows in Your ways! I won't walk in step with the wicked, nor share the sinner's way, nor be found sitting in the scorner's seat. My pleasure and passion remain true to the Word of You Lord. I meditate day and night in the true revelation of Your light. I stand firm like a flourishing tree planted by Your design, deeply rooted by the brooks of bliss, bearing fruit in every season of my life. I am never dry, never fainting, ever blessed, and ever prosperous.

Psalms 1:1-3

Father, I long for more revelation of your truth, for I love the light of your word as I meditate on your decrees. In the middle of the night, I awake to give thanks to you because of all your revelation-light; it is so right and true! Day and night your Words are always on my lips, Your words fill my life with prosperity and success and I am forever thankful!

Psalms 119:48, 62 Joshua 1:8

O God of my life, I'm lovesick for you in this weary wilderness. I thirst with the deepest longings to love you more, with cravings in my heart that can't be described. Such yearning grips my soul for you, my God! I lie awake at night thinking of you and reflecting on how you help me like a father their beloved child. I sing through the night under your splendor-shadow, offering up to you my songs of delight and joy!

Psalms 63:1, 6-7

I thank you, Lord that as I meditate on your word that my soul prospers and this means that in every other area of my life will prosper as I stay focused on You and your precious truths. My heart is full of thanksgiving.

3 John 1:2

Lord, I commit to you to be an example for all to see of your faithfulness and truth living through my life. May authentic love be my banner as I diligently remain in your word meditating and devouring Your truths and teaching them to others.
1 Timothy 4:11-14

Visualization

Thank you, Jesus, that you helped people in the past and today to understand truths of your word through parables to ignite the visual

side of mankind. I thank you that I can still today receive your truths in image form. I commit my imagination for your glory and purposes to see in word pictures, visions, and dreams.
Matthew 13:34

Father, I ask you to continue to pour out your Spirit on everybody and cause our sons and daughters to prophesy, and our young men to see visions, and the old men to experience Your dreams!

Acts 2:17

Father, I thank you for the revelation that for although I live in the natural realm, I don't wage a military campaign employing human weapons, using manipulation to achieve my aims. Instead, my spiritual weapons are energized with divine power to dismantle the defences behind which people hide effectively. I can demolish every deceptive fantasy that opposes God and break through every arrogant attitude that is raised up in defiance of Your true knowledge. I capture, like prisoners of war, every thought and insist that it bow in obedience to the Jesus the Anointed One."
2 Corinthians 10:3-5

Take thoughts captive

Father, I thank you for the revelation that for although I live in the natural realm, I don't wage a military campaign employing human weapons, using manipulation to achieve my aims. Instead, my spiritual weapons are energized with divine power to effectively dismantle the defenses behind which people hide. I can demolish every deceptive fantasy that opposes God and break through every arrogant attitude that is raised up in defiance of Your true knowledge. I capture, like prisoners of war, every thought and insist that it bow in obedience to the Jesus the Anointed One. I am armed with dynamic weaponry; I stand ready to punish any trace of rebellion, as soon as I choose complete obedience.

2 Corinthians 10:3-6

Father, I thank you for giving me the living Word, it is full of energy, and it pierces me more sharply than any two-edged sword. It penetrates to the very core of my being where soul and spirit, bone and marrow meet! It enables me to interpret and reveal my true thoughts and secret motives of my heart. And not a creature exists that is concealed from Your sight, but all things are open and exposed and revealed to You.

Hebrews 4:12-13

Father, I know the plans and thoughts that You have for me, Your plans for peace and well-being and not for disaster. I know that when I embrace the truth, it releases true freedom into my life, heals my wounds, heals my heart and gives me hope for the future.

Jeremiah 29:11, Psalms 147:3, John 8:32

Lords I take my thoughts captive that are not filled with life and hope and exchange them for your truths. I believe I will grow and prosper in my soul. I commit to this as Hope deferred makes the heart sick, so I set my eyes firmly fixed on things above. Amen
Proverbs 13:12

Rest in Christ

Father, I thank you for giving me full and complete rest, which allows me to cease from my own works and follow Your example. Just as You celebrated Your finished work and rested in them. So then I must give my all and be eager to experience Your abundant rest filled life.

Hebrews 4:9-11

Praise God that there are great rewards for resting in You and laboring into that rest. However, I thank you Lord that I can only do this with faith and believing that when You speak truth, it will come to pass in my life. I choose to passionately seek you and your ways no matter the obstacle and no matter when what I see with my eyes

do not line up with your truth.
Hebrews 11:6

Set a guard

Father, I have made a covenant with my eyes; I refuse to gaze on that which is vulgar. I despise works of evil people and anything that moves my heart away from you. I will not let evil hold me in its grip. Help me turn my eyes away from illusions so that I pursue only that which is true; drench my soul with life as I walk in your paths.

Job 31:1a, Psalms 101:3, Psalms 119:37

Lord, I make a choice today to remove distractions from my life that dishonor You. But not just dishonor as all things are permissible but not beneficial therefore help me to see those things in my life that do not benefit the plans You have for me. I refuse to serve two masters I choose to serve the One and only true God, and that is You, Yahweh.
Matthew 6:23-24

Help me Lord to see areas in my life that have been sinful. I choose to obedient to You and willingly let go of all deceptions and lies the enemy has been trying to seduce me with. I commit my ways to You as it is not I that lives but Christ that lives in me. My body is your temple and commit it to You again today.
Matthew 5:29

Lord, I walk in faith today. Faith comes from hearing from You and doing what Your Word requires me to do. As I renew my mind, I trust that transformation by faith is built up in me.
Romans 10:17

Father, I open my heart fully to your ways and words by paying careful attention to my heart that it is not closed or hard-hearted. I

know that as I diligently listen to you, I know that revelation is progressive and I will receive truths that overflow in abundance. I love you. In Jesus' name, Amen.
Luke 8:18

Lord, I will be a doer of your Word as I integrate Faith actions into my life. I know that You will guide me in all truth. I refuse to deceive myself and believe that just knowing your Word is being a doer of it. That reading the Word is a lifestyle choice but doing Your word is where my faith is. I will not be deceived and forget what I read and study and continue in this study and mind renewal process I will see more and more clearly, and I will be blessed in all that I do.
James 1:19-27

Journaling

Father, I will stand at my guard post And station myself on the tower; And I will keep watch to see what You will say to me, And what answer I will give as Your spokesman when I am reproved. I will follow your commands and Write the vision plainly So that anyone who reads it will be able to run with it. Habakkuk 2:1-2

Total Immersion

Father, I immerse myself in your teaching and meditate on them constantly. Your Word has become so real in my life that it bears fruit and everyone can see my progress. I give careful attention to my spiritual life and cherished every truth, for living by Your Word releases an even more abundant life inside me. I am continually being renewed in the spirit of my mind; I put on my new self, created after Your likeness in true righteousness and holiness."
1 Timothy 4:15-16, Ephesians 4:23-24

Father, how can I listen to Your Word of Truth and not respond to it, for that would be the essence of self-deception. So I let Your Word become like poetry written and fulfilled by my life! I listen to Your

Word and live out the message. I'm thankful I can look in the mirror and perceive how You see me in the mirror of Your Word so that I never go out and forget my divine origin. I set my gaze deeply into the perfecting law of liberty and am fascinated by and respond to the truth I hear; I am strengthened by it—I experience God's blessing in all that I do!"

James 1:22-25

Father, because I have been crucified with Christ, my life is hidden in you! You can now call me Your chosen treasure, a chosen race, a royal priesthood, a holy nation, a person for Your own possession. I am able to proclaim Your excellency because You called me out of darkness into Your marvelous light.

Colossians 3:3, 1 Peter 2:9

Serving Others/Intercession

As I walk in being a doer of Your word I believe that truly knowing and believing what You are teaching me in exemplified in how well I can give back to others. Lord bring people around me that I can share truths that you have showed me. I know that this is such a powerful way to renew my mind and that it will flow back to me in abundance, pressed down and shaken.

Luke 6:38

Just like Jesus who did not come to be served but to serve I shall do the same. Open doors Father so that I can give to others and serve others. Bless me in abundance, so I can be an abundant blessing to all.

Mark 10:45

Lord, lead me to stay committed to accountability in this journey. I know that love empowers me to carry the burdens of my brother or sister. As we cover one another in prayer and counsel strengthen us to stay the course. As we pray together in your name, I am grateful to You because You are right here with us now, even in our midst. In Jesus' Name Amen.

Matthew 18:19-20

Father God, Empower me to cling close to you and your word so that I won't sin. Help me to remove all dishonest thinking, speaking, and behavior; so that I will be a person of integrity, honesty and truth before all people and the angels, as a testimony to me belonging to you and your church.
Ephesians 4:25

Mind Renewal/Transformation

My Heavenly Father, thank you that I can present my body as a living sacrifice. Let everything I do with my body be a holy and acceptable love gift to you, because of your great mercy. I worship you, I love you, Jesus… you are my Lord. Holy Spirit you help me to renew my mind so that I will not live a life that reflects the world, but a transformed life that reflects heaven. This mind we build together in partnership, will know what the will of God is, which is always good, acceptable and perfect.
Romans 12:1-2

My wonderful Father, I receive the teachings of Jesus Christ as truth to me. Holy Spirit, help me to put off everything that is of the old un-renewed self. I receive your power, person, and guidance into my mind, to govern my mind, direct my mind, and change every spiritual foundation that my mind is connected to and make it your foundation. Holy Spirit I choose to give you full control so that I can put on the new self fully, my heavenly self. I thank you that my renewed self looks like your image, thinks like Jesus and is righteous and holy.

With your help Father, I refuse to let anger cause sin in my life; I refuse to let falsehood develop in me, Father; let your truth develop in me mightily. I praise you, God that you have given me the power by your Spirit and Word to give no opportunity to the devil, the enemy has no victory, Jesus has the victory, and I share in His victory because of the cross, and the resurrection.

Thank you, Jesus, for sealing me with your precious Holy Spirit. Amen.

Ephesians 4:21-30

FELLOWSHIP PRAYERS - IHOPKC

Mike Bickle - IHOPKC

I. F-E-L-L-O-W-S-H-I-P

A. A prayer list is a simple tool that helps us to focus in our prayer times. I have identified ten prayers to pray daily to receive strength in my inner man using the acronym F-E-L-L-O-W-S-H-I-P.

B. *F*: Fear of God

1. The Lord promised to put the fear of God into the hearts of His people (Jer. 32:40). He will do this more as we ask the Spirit to unite our heart to His heart and fill it with awe (Ps. 86:11).

⁴⁰I will put <u>My fear in their hearts</u> so that they will not depart from Me. (Jer. 32:40)

¹¹<u>Unite my heart</u> to fear Your name. (Ps. 86: 11)

¹³The Lord...you shall hallow; <u>let Him be your fear</u>, and let Him be your dread. (Isa. 8:13)

2. It is far easier to resist compromise when we feel even a small measure of the fear, or awe, of God in our hearts. Ask Him to cause you to delight in the fear of the Lord (Isa. 11:3) and to strike your heart with the majesty and awesome dread of God (Isa. 8:13).

3. *Prayer*: Father, release the spirit of the fear of God into my heart. Strike my heart with greater understanding of Your Majesty that I may live in awe before You. Unite my heart to Your heart and Word, and cause me to delight in the fear of God.

C. *E*: Endurance

1. In the Bible, the words *endurance*, *perseverance*, and *patience* are often interchangeable. These words speak of being faithful in our God-given assignments and refusing to quit even when facing great pressures. Holy-Spirit-empowered endurance enables us to seek and serve the Lord faithfully with all our strength for decades without drawing back.

¹¹Being strengthened with all power...so that you may have <u>great endurance</u> and <u>patience</u>. (Col. 1:11, NIV)

³May the Lord direct your hearts into … the <u>patience</u> [endurance] **of Christ. (2 Thessalonians 3:5)**

2. David and Jesus spoke of being consumed with zeal for God's house (Ps. 69:9; Jn. 2:17). Another way to ask for endurance is by asking God to impart zeal to your heart. Zeal and endurance are two sides of one coin. It takes God's power touching our heart and mind to keep us from drawing back in our zeal and wholeheartedness. Ask the Lord to give you endurance or zeal to be faithful, especially in the difficult and dry seasons of life.

⁹…for zeal for Your house consumes me [David]**…(Ps. 69:9)**

3. **Prayer**: Father, strengthen my heart with endurance, that I may faithfully do Your will with zeal and diligence and never draw back in any way in my pursuit of the deeper things of Your heart and will. Give me endurance to fast regularly. Direct my heart into the patience, or endurance, in which Jesus walked (2 Thessalonians. 3:5). Give me strength to follow through in my commitments to You and to fulfill my ministry calling even when it is difficult or small.

D. **L**: Love

1. The Spirit's first agenda is to establish the first commandment in first place in us that we will love Jesus with all our strength (Mt. 22:37). Jesus asked the Father to impart the very love that He has for Jesus into our hearts (Jn. 17:26). It "takes God to love God." The grace to receive God's love and to love Him back is the greatest gift the Spirit imparts to us (Rom. 5:5).

²⁶…that the love with which You [the Father] **loved Me** [Jesus] **may be in them. (Jn. 17:26)**

⁵The love of God has been <u>poured out in our hearts</u> by the Holy Spirit. (Rom. 5:5)

2. In asking to abound in love, we are actually asking for the Spirit to inspire us in four ways— for greater understanding of God's love for us; for the Spirit to tenderize our hearts so that we abound in love for Jesus; to cause love for others to abound in our hearts; to love ourselves in the grace of God. Jesus commanded us, "Love your neighbor *as yourself*" (Mt. 22:39).

⁹I pray, that <u>your love may abound</u> still more… (Phil. 1:9)

¹²May the Lord make you increase and <u>abound in love</u> to one another. (1 Thessalonians 3:12)

3. **Prayer**: Father, pour out Your love in my heart by the Spirit that I may overflow in love back to You and to others (Rom. 5:5). Impart Your own love for Jesus into my heart (Jn. 17:26). Allow me to comprehend Jesus' love for me (Jn. 15:9; Eph. 3:18). Let me see myself through Your eyes so that I may love who You created me to be (Ps. 139:13-15).

E. **L**: Light of glory

1. On the day of Paul's conversion he saw Jesus and His glory in a great light (Acts 22:6-11).

> **6"...suddenly a <u>great light</u> from heaven shone around me...¹¹And since I could not see for the <u>glory of that light</u>, being led by the hand...I came into Damascus." (Acts 22:6, 11)**

2. Moses prayed to see God's glory, and afterward, his face shone with the light of God's glory (Ex. 33:18; 34:29). We also can ask to encounter the realm of God's glory. Jesus spoke of an open heaven in which His disciples would see angels (Jn. 1:51). Ask Him to shine the light of His countenance (Ps. 4:6) on your heart in such a way that you experience the supernatural realm of His glory, including receiving dreams and visions and seeing angels, etc. (Acts 2:17).

> **⁵¹And He [Jesus] said to him, "Most assuredly..., hereafter <u>you</u> <u>shall see heaven open, and the angels of God</u> ascending and descending upon the Son of Man." (Jn. 1:51)**

> **¹⁷... in the last days...I will pour out of My Spirit on <u>all flesh</u>; your sons and daughters <u>shall prophesy</u>, your young men shall <u>see visions</u>, your old men <u>shall dream dreams</u>. (Acts 2:17)**

3. **Prayer**: Father, let me see the light of Your glory and give me supernatural encounters—dreams, visions, angelic visitations, manifestations of Your glory and light—even as You gave to Moses, Isaiah, Ezekiel, Paul, John, and the disciples on the Day of Pentecost (Ex. 33-34; Isa. 6; Ezek. 1; Acts 2; Acts 9; Rev. 1).

F. **O**: One thing

1. It is essential to spend time with the Lord—to be a person of "one thing" as King David was. David revealed his primary life focus when he prayed that the "one thing" he desired all the days of his life was to behold the beauty of the Lord, and to inquire in His temple (Ps. 27:4).

<u>⁴One thing I have desired</u>...all the days of my life, to behold the beauty of the Lord...
(Ps. 27:4)

2. Mary of Bethany "sat at Jesus' feet and heard His word" (Lk 10:39). Jesus explained to her sister Martha, "One thing is needed, and Mary has chosen that good part" (Lk. 10:42).

⁴²But <u>one thing is needed</u>, and Mary has chosen that good part. (Lk. 10:42)

3. We must intentionally set our hearts to be a "person of one thing." We ask the Spirit to help us not to lose this focus by intervening to speak to our heart when drifting from a "one thing lifestyle." Ask Him to speak to you using Scripture, others, dreams, or His still, small voice.

4. **Prayer**: Father, I commit to live as a "person of one thing." Help me to sit regularly at Your feet to behold Your beauty as David and Mary of Bethany did. Strengthen my desire in this, and help me to maintain a lifestyle of regular time with You in Your Word. When I lose this focus, get my attention and send Your Word to deliver me of a divided heart.

G. **W**: Worthy

1. Paul prayed that God would count the saints worthy to fulfill all of His will (2 Thess. 1:11). He emphasized that he *always* prayed this for the saints—he understood how important it was. Walking worthy is *not the same as seeking to be worthy by earning our forgiveness*. Rather, it is about experiencing grace in such a consistent way that we walk with a *worthy response* to God that prepares us to walk in the fullness of our calling, thus fulfilling all His goodness.

¹¹We pray always for you that our God would <u>count you worthy</u> of this calling, and fulfill all the good pleasure of His goodness and the work of faith with power. (2 Thes. 1:11)

2. Too many believers come up short of what God has invited them to walk in because of their halfhearted responses and choices. Jesus exhorted us to pray that we may be counted worthy to *escape the snare of stumbling* (Lk 21:34-36). Walking worthy of our calling includes being strengthened to escape the snare of compromise so that we stand in victory before God.

34"Take heed...lest your <u>hearts be weighed down</u> with carousing, drunkenness, and cares of this life, and that Day come on you unexpectedly. 35For it will come <u>as a snare</u> on all those who dwell on the face of the earth. 36Watch therefore, and pray always that you may be counted worthy to <u>escape all these things</u>...to stand before the Son of Man." (Lk. 21:34-36)

3. *Prayer*: Father, strengthen my heart so that I walk in a measure of faith and obedience that is worthy of who You are and of Your calling on my life. Help me to walk worthy of You by escaping all compromise. Prepare me to walk in the highest things You have called me to. Help me to live free of the snare of compromise so that I will walk blamelessly so to stand before You victoriously with the testimony that I sought to obey You with all my heart.

H. *S*: Speech

1. Speech is a significant issue in our lives. When our speech comes under the leadership of the Spirit, our entire inner man will also come under His leadership.

2If anyone does not stumble in word, he is a <u>perfect man</u>, able also to bridle the whole body. (Jas 3:2)

2. Paul spoke about not grieving the Holy Spirit by our speech (Eph. 4:29-30).

29<u>Let no corrupt word proceed out of your mouth</u>, but what is good for necessary edification... 30And do not grieve the Holy Spirit... (Eph. 4:29-30)

3. The subject of speech was on David's "prayer list"—he asked the Lord to help him control his speech so that his words would be pleasing to God (Ps. 19:14).

14Let the words of <u>my mouth</u> and the meditation of my heart be acceptable in Your sight. (Ps. 19:14)

4. David purposed that he would not sin with his speech, so he asked the Lord to set a guard over his mouth (Ps. 17:3; 141:3).

[3]...I have purposed that my mouth shall not transgress. (Ps. 17:3)

[3]Set a guard, O Lord, <u>over my mouth</u>; keep watch over the door of my lips. (Ps. 141:3)

[1]I will guard my ways, <u>lest I sin with my tongue</u>; I will restrain my mouth with a muzzle. (Ps. 39:1)

5. **Prayer**: Father, set a guard over my lips and help me to speak words that are pleasing to You. Free me from defensive, angry, foolish, sensual, or impure speech. Keep me from quenching the Spirit with my words. I set my heart not to sin with my speech.

I. **H**: Humility

1. Jesus called us to *learn from Him* about walking in humility or lowliness (Mt. 11:29).

[29]Take My yoke...and <u>learn from Me</u>, for I am gentle and <u>lowly in heart</u>. (Mt. 11:29)

2. Paul called us to let the "mind of Christ" or His mindset of humility be in us (Phil. 2:3-5).

[3]Let nothing be done through selfish ambition or conceit, but <u>in lowliness of mind</u> let each esteem others better than himself. [4]Let each of you look out not only for his own interests, but also for the interests of others. [5]<u>Let this mind be in you which was also in Christ</u>... (Phil. 2:3-5)

J. **Prayer**: Jesus, teach me how to walk in Your yoke of humility (lowliness of heart). I set my heart to learn humility from You, gaining insight that will result in the transformation of my attitudes, speech, and actions. Give me wisdom about how to carry my heart in humility.

I: Insight

1. The Spirit came to teach us all things—to give us insight or wisdom as He fills us with the knowledge of His will for each area of our life so we are able to walk in partnership with His heart (Col. 1:9-10). The Lord's desire is to give His people wisdom so that they are fruitful in every endeavor to obey Him and that they grow in or experience the knowledge of His heart in the process.

2. The insight that He gives His people is intended to lead and teach them how to walk in agreement with His heart so that they enjoy friendship and partnership with Him. He gives wisdom on how to steward time, money, careers, ministry, health, relationships, etc. He will give us insight into what is on His heart for cities and nations and for our generation.

⁹...to ask that you may be filled with the knowledge of His will [insight] **in all wisdom and spiritual understanding; ¹⁰that you may walk worthy of the Lord, fully pleasing Him, being fruitful in every good work and increasing in the knowledge of God.... (Col. 1:9-10)**

²⁶But the Helper, the Holy Spirit...He will teach you all things... (Jn. 14:26)

3. **Prayer**: Father, give me insight into Your Word, will, and ways. Give me wisdom about how to walk in intimacy with You in every area of my life, including my finances, schedule, emotions, physical body (diet, health), relationships (home, office, ministry), future, fears, etc. What are You thinking and feeling about me and my life, city, nation, and generation?

K. **P**: Peace and joy

1. The Spirit desires to guard our hearts and minds with supernatural peace. In Philippians 4:7, the "heart" speaks of our emotions. We do not have to live troubled by jealousy, rejection, anxiety, or fear, or with minds that are filled with turmoil, confusion, and indecision. If we regularly ask for peace and joy in specific areas of our lives, we will receive more of them.

⁷The peace of God...will guard your hearts and minds through Christ Jesus. (Phil. 4:7)

¹³Now may the God of hope fill you with all joy and peace in believing... (Rom. 15:13)

2. **Prayer**: Father, strengthen my heart with supernatural peace in areas in which I feel rejection, fear, or anxiety; strengthen my mind so I may overcome turmoil, confusion, and indecision.

FORMS WORKSHEETS & TEMPLATES

FORMS, WORKSHEETS & TEMPLATES

The weekly renewing the mind trackers and copies of all these worksheets can be found on www.sophiatucker.com under the tab RTM101

SCRIPTURE JOURNAL TEMPLATE

TOPIC: _____

Steps

1. Write down all the thoughts, feelings, opinions and emotions you are currently feeling.
2. Number each entry
3. Pray and ask the Lord to reveal to you His truth about this situation
4. Identify the main issue you are facing. Is it guilt? Condemnation, Gluttony, Fear, Insecurity?
5. Visit a site like www.openbible.info and type in the main issue and you will get scriptures that apply
6. Allow the Holy Spirit to lead you in which scripture speaks the truth about each lie and write out the scripture or reference and any notes you have
7. Write an affirmation or scripture prayer for each lie
8. Take the list of prayers and affirmations and renew your mind with them during the day.
9. How do you know your mind has been renewed? When the old thoughts are not dictating your day to day actions, but your new truth dictates your life.

Thoughts, Feelings, Opinions or Emotions	Scripture Notes	Affirmation/Prayer
I have just blown it I have just eaten this whole bag of cookies God is not going to be pleased with me	Jeremiah 31:3 Romans 8: 1 There is no condemnation for me.	Thank you, Lord that no matter the mistake I may have made. You are pleased with me, and there is no condemnation for me.

Steps to use the 'Think on' Model

1. Write the topic you want to meditate on.
   Is it a person that has offended you? A situation that has happened that has led you to fall into anger or dismay about. We are going to first write this out.

2. Then we are going to pray and give this area to God and ask Him to show us the truth about this situation

3. Next, we are going to look at each area that the word tells us to meditate on and decide what is:
   TRUE – HONORABLE – RIGHT – PURE – LOVELY – ADMIRABLE – VIRTUOUS – PRAISEWORTHY

4. Once we have the list of our thoughts we are going to write a statement/affirmation for each and we are going to take each and spend time speaking these out as truths every day or several times a day until we have healing and peace about this situation, evidence that our mind is renewed on this matter.

Note. Every time a situation comes up you are going to meditate on the statements.

TOPIC: _____

Think on these things Reckon (calculate, judge and conclude), reason, decide, think, meditate on.	Thoughts	Statement of Truth
True Whatever is worthy of credit, truthful and when tested it would without doubt, proven to be fact?		
Honourable/Noble Whatever is dignified about a person or situation?		
Just/Right Whatever is just or right before the eyes of God, His standard or righteous in His eyes. Whatever is correct about a thing or person?		
Pure Whatever is pure, innocent, sacred, and perfect		

Lovely Whatever is pleasing, acceptable, agreeable, and great, cherished, highly prized. Anything that is worthy to have and embrace.		
Good Report/Admirable Something worthy of praise or commendable about a person or thing.		
Virtuous The excellence of a person (in body or mind) or of a thing, an eminent endowment, property or quality, a good or gracious matter or act. Anything worthy of praise.		
Praiseworthy Enthusiastic acknowledgment of anything that deserves praise. Recognizing good in a person or situation		

THINK ON MODEL

THINK ON MODEL

See below an example of a Think On Model.

Meditate on These Things

8 Finally, brethren, whatever things are true, whatever things are noble, whatever things are just, whatever things are pure, whatever things are lovely, whatever things are of good report, if there is any virtue and if there is anything praiseworthy—meditate on these things.

9 The things which you learned and received and heard and saw in me, these do, and the God of peace will be with you.

TRUE

- I have the boldness of Christ living in me

- I have soundness of mind

- God is with me every step of the way

- I have peace that guards my heart

- There is therefore now no condemnation for those who are in Christ Jesus

- Your enabling grace is upon my life

NOBLE

- Jesus righteousness is upon me

- I sit in the royal courts of heaven with my Father

- God is faithful and my Great defender

- God's love for me is never-ending

- He wills for me to succeed

- According to Proverbs 31. I am of high noble positioning, and my worth is above Rubies

- And my God will supply every need of yours according to his riches in glory in Christ Jesus

- Or do you not know that your body is a temple of the Holy Spirit within you, whom you have from God? You are not your own, for you were bought with a price. So glorify God in your body.

JUST

- God, You are just and fair and judge my heart well.

- You are just Lord and so any trial I face You turn it all around for MY good

- Every promise You have made You are faithful to accomplish it.

- And will not [our just] God defend and protect and avenge His elect (His chosen ones), who cry to Him day and night? Will He defer them and delay help on their behalf? I tell you, He will defend and protect and avenge them speedily. LUKE 18:7-8

PURE

- The fear of the LORD is pure, enduring forever. The decrees of the LORD are firm, and all of them are righteous.

- I take every worrisome thought captive to the pure truth of God.

- Lord, I place my focus and attention on You, and I know You will guard my heart and keep me in perfect peace.

LOVELY

- I thank you, Lord for in me you have placed a fighting spirit.

- I praise God that as I will pass this will be another great testimony of your faithfulness towards me.

- You cherish me as Your beloved.

- You love me with a relentless deep love that is unconditional.

- My soul, body, and spirit bask in the beauty of Your countenance and the Word.

GOOD REPORT

- HALLELUJAH LORD your report is I shall be transformed

- Hallelujah Lord Your report that there is more on my side.

- HALLELUJAH PERFECT LOVE CASTS OUT FEAR!!

- HALLELUJAH You have also given me the shield of Your salvation, And Your right hand upholds me, And Your gentleness makes me great.

- But thanks be to God, who always leads us in triumph in Christ, and manifests through us the sweet aroma of the knowledge of Him in every place.

- But thanks be to God, who gives us the victory through our Lord Jesus Christ.

- HALLELUJAH The horse is prepared for the day of battle, But victory belongs to the LORD.

- And we know that God causes all things to work together for good to those who love God, to those who are called according to His purpose.

MIRROR EXERCISES

Mirror Exercises

(Print these and put somewhere near your mirror. Look at yourself in the mirror and speak these truths daily)

Father God, I am a believer, I believe every word You've said

All of Your Words are true so that I can have total faith in God

What Your word says I can do, I can and will do with all my heart

I believe what your word says about me

I'm going to do what it says I can do

It's not I who live, but Christ lives in me, so my faith is effective, He is in me

The old me is gone. I am new; I was raised up with Jesus to sit with Him

I will live and declare the gospel and exalt the word of the Lord

I am free, and the Lord fights my battles on my behalf - victory is mine

God provides all my needs by His riches and glory

I have the mind of Christ; I renew my mind daily to it

I pull down all that exalts itself against the true knowledge of God

I refuse thoughts of fear, failure, and defeat; I only think thoughts of victory

I meditate on God's word day and night, and I am transformed

I love Your presence O Lord, Your love and hope dwell richly in my heart

The power of your Word makes me live with confidence

Whatever I ask in prayer, I receive by faith, because I am not double minded

I daily pull down every toxic thought that does not align with the Word of God

I boldly declare the Word of the Lord. So I face all situations with peace

My spirit takes the lead today

THE POWER
OF A FOCUSED LIFE – IHOPKC

"THE POWER OF A FOCUSED LIFE"

RENEWING THE MIND 101 STUDY WORKSHEET

STEP 1: Vision

Write out your overall vision for this journey? (What is your overall vision for this journey you are on)

_____
_____
_____
_____
_____
_____
_____
_____
_____

1. **What would you want those who knew you best to say about you when you have reached your goal?**

Indicate specific people and the statements you would like to hear each of them say about you.

Person: Jesus

Statement about you:

_____
_____
_____
_____
_____
_____
_____

Person:

_____
_____
_____
_____

Statement about you:

_____

_____

_____

_____

_____

_____

Person:

_____

_____

_____

_____

Statement about you:

_____

_____

_____

_____

Person:

_____

_____

_____

Statement about you:

_____

_____

_____

_____

STEP 2: Goals: Write your short term goals (during the study) and long term (after the study)

II. **Spiritually** (bible study, prayer time, accountability, mind renewal, fasting, etc.)

Short-term goals:

1. _____
_____
_____

2. _____
_____
_____

3. _____
_____
_____

Long-term goals:

1. _____
_____
_____
_____

2. _____
_____
_____

3. _____
_____
_____

III. **Relationally** (family, friends, accountability partners etc.)

Short-term goals:

1.

_____

_____

_____

2.

_____

_____

_____

3.

_____

_____

_____

Long-term goals:

1.

_____

_____

_____

2.

_____

_____

_____

3.

_____

_____

_____

IV. **Physically** (exercise, health, boundaries, etc.)

Short-term goals:

1.

_____

_____

_____

2.

_____

_____

_____

Long-term goals:

1.

_____

_____

_____

2.

_____

_____

_____

STEP 3: Action Plans: Describe your specific activities you will do to accomplish these goals.

V. **Spiritually** (bible study, prayer time, accountability, mind renewal, fasting, etc.)

Short-term goals:

_____

_____

_____

Action steps:

_____

_____

_____

Long-terms goal:

_____

_____

_____

Action steps:

_____

_____

_____

Relationally (family, friends, accountability partner etc.)

Short-term goals:

_____

_____

_____

Action steps:

_____

_____

_____

Long-term goals:

_____

_____

_____

Action steps:

_____

_____

_____

A. **Physically** (exercise, health, boundaries, etc)

Short-term goals:

_____
_____
_____

Action steps:

_____
_____
_____
_____
_____
_____

Long-term goals:

_____
_____
_____

Action steps:

_____
_____
_____

STEP 4: Scheduling Your Time: What specific times will you implement your action plans? ***This is the most crucial part of turning vision into reality.***

Please see a schedule template on the following page.

Firstly take the time to fill out the "Actual Schedule" based on a typical 24 hours.

Then complete the "Preferred Schedule" of how you would prefer a typical 24 hour day would be. Ensuring those times of mind renewal & prayer is included.

Personal Day Assessment (Actual)

Time	Task	Notes
4.00		
5.00		
6.00		
7.00		
8.00		
9.00		
10.00		
11.00		
12.00		
13.00		
14.00		
15.00		
16.00		
17.00		
18.00		
19.00		
20.00		
21.00		
22.00		
23.00		
24.00		

Personal Day Assessment (Preferred)

Time	Task	Notes
4.00		
5.00		
6.00		
7.00		
8.00		
9.00		
10.00		
11.00		
12.00		
13.00		
14.00		
15.00		
16.00		
17.00		
18.00		
19.00		
20.00		
21.00		
22.00		
23.00		
24.00		

Guidance Notes by Mike Bickle – IHOP KC

Vision: Our vision is most effective when we have measurable goals and an action plan with a schedule. We need a clear vision with measurable goals as well as an action plan, a series of practical steps that help us fulfill our goals. We establish a schedule that is in agreement with our action plan, goals, and vision.

Life Goals: We set measurable goals or objectives for each area of life to help us walk out our vision. We need long-term goals and short-term goals

Action plan: We need an action plan for each long-term and short-term goal (in each area of life). Our action plan is the series of small steps we do that help us fulfil our goals. Goals that do not have an action plan will not be fulfilled. Therefore taking time to write an action plan is essential. If you can't write out your vision, action plan, and schedule, then mostly likely you do not have them.

Schedule: Make a schedule for each action plan to provide focus for your priorities. A schedule is a target to aim at, or a "road map" to help us keep on track. In making a schedule, we must allow for emergencies and unexpected things. I do not expect to keep my schedule 100%. We will benefit greatly if we keep our schedule even 80% of the time.

Good is the enemy of the best.

We can easily get caught up in the tyranny of the urgent instead of living with focus on our purpose. If you do not determine your schedule, then others will.

In seeking to walk in the fullness of our calling and destiny in God, we must clearly identify our vision or life purpose—what is it that we most want to be or do? Without a vision the people "perish" or they miss out on their life destiny. Without a vision, we squander our destiny. To "cast off restraint" means to not use our resources in a way that helps us walk out our life vision.

Where there is no vision, the people perish.
(Pro. 29:18, KJV)

Where there is no revelation, the people cast off restraint. (Prov. 29:18, NKJV)

Time is one of our most valuable resources. Money is power, but time is life. We "redeem" our time by wisely using it in ways that are "redemptive," or useful to God's purpose in our life.

Awake, you who sleep...Christ will shine on you. 15 See then that you walk wisely, not as fools but as wise, 16 redeeming the time, because the days are evil. (Eph. 5:14-16)

THE END

38986077R00148

Made in the USA
Middletown, DE
13 March 2019